Got Teens?

JILL SAVAGE & PAM FARREL

HARVEST HOUSE PUBLISHERS

EUGENE, OREGON

Published in association with the literary agency of Alive Communications, Inc., 7680 Goddard Street, Ste #200, Colorado Springs, CO 80920.

The cartoons in this book are © Zits Partnership. Reprinted with special permission of King Features Syndicate.

Cover by Terry Dugan Design, Minneapolis, Minnesota

GOT TEENS?
Copyright © 2005 by Jill Savage and Pam Farrel
Published by Harvest House Publishers
Eugene, Oregon 97402
www.harvesthousepublishers.com

Library of Congress Cataloging-in-Publication Data

Savage, Jill, 1964–
    Got teens? / Jill Savage and Pam Farrel.
       p. cm.
    Includes bibliographical references (p.   ).
    ISBN-13: 978-0-7369-1499-4 (pbk.)
    ISBN-10: 0-7369-1499-4 (pbk.)
    1. Child rearing—Religious aspects—Christianity. 2. Parenting—Religious aspects—Christianity. 3. Parent and teenager—Religious aspects—Christianity. 4. Mothers—Religious life. I. Farrel, Pam, 1959– II. Title.
    BV4529.18.S24 2005
    248.8'45—dc22   2005004566

Printed in the United States of America

05 06 07 08 09 10 11 12 / VP-MS / 10 9 8 7 6 5 4 3 2 1

Acknowledgments
from Jill

No book is a solo project. Dozens of people have worked together to create a resource we hope will encourage moms for many years to come. Special thanks goes to...

...*the women of Hearts at Home.* You have shared your stories, your struggles, and your desire for a resource that will help you be the best parent you can be for your teens. Thank you for taking the profession of motherhood seriously.

...*the volunteer staff that make Hearts at Home happen.* You will work hard to put this book in the hands of moms who need it. Thank you for giving your time and energy to promote and encourage the profession of motherhood.

...*the Harvest House staff.* This has been one of the most enjoyable book projects I've ever worked on. Thank you for believing in the ministry of Hearts at Home, the message of this book, and the power of the written word. You guys know how to make the publishing process absolutely enjoyable!

...*my friends Becky, Tonya, and Angie.* You each contributed to making this project happen—you are incredible! Thank you to Becky's friend Laury, who took the time to go through hundreds of *Zits* cartoons to find just the right ones! And thank you, Kyle Thede, for loaning us your precious *Zits* books!

...*Mary Steinke and the Hearts at Home publishing team.* Your work behind the scenes is vital to making this project the best it can be!

...*my coauthor, Pam.* Writing with you has been a joy, as has been getting to know you and Bill across the miles. Thank you for your hard work and your encouragement. You are a cheerleader of people, girlfriend!

...*my children, Anne, Evan, Erica, Kolya, and Austin.* Thank you for letting me share your stories to encourage other families, and thank you for being willing to eat a little more frozen pizza than usual! I love you, and I think you are incredible kids!

...*my husband, Mark.* I think we're really catching on to the steps in the dance of book projects. Thank you for your encouragement, feedback, and partnership in parenting. I love you more every day!

...*my Friend, Lord, and Savior, Jesus Christ.* Thank You for loving me through my teen years, for welcoming me back to You with open arms, and for giving me the opportunity to encourage others with Your truth!

Acknowledgments
from Pam

To three outstanding sons, Brock, Zach, and Caleb.
Being your mom is an incredible, amazing privilege.
I am a better person for the experience,
and I am grateful to God
because He "wows" me every day with each of you!
Psalm 84:11—you know it, you live it.
I know I will keep hearing a good report.
You make your mama proud!

To Bill, no one ever had a better partner in parenting.
I love teaming with you.

To Jill, the fantastic Hearts at Home staff,
and the Hearts at Home moms.
Knowing you has made my life richer, better, and stronger.
May God shine His grace and favor on you.

Contents

Introduction

Between the two of us, we have six teenagers. We've learned many lessons over the years by trial and error. Sometimes we feel equipped and empowered to lead our teenagers, and sometimes we are begging God for wisdom because we don't have a clue how to handle a situation we are facing.

Our firstborns have *guinea pig* written all over them. Bless their hearts—they helped us learn valuable lessons about leading kids through the wonderful years of transition from childhood to adulthood. But even with some experience under our belt, we know that every child is unique and has his or her own way of processing life, making choices, and forging into adulthood.

Through our successes and our failures, we hope to share with you how to show love, give direction, and use discernment in raising your teens. We hope you also find lots of practical help to answer daily questions like *Should I let him go with his friends to the lake?* or *Who should pay for the gas in the car?* We want to provide emotional support as you navigate the ever-changing landscape of the 12 to 20 window. We also hope to help you get connected and stay connected to your child's Creator because God has the operator's manual for your tweens (almost teenagers) and teens.

Introductions are in order for you to get to know us a little better. Jill is the Founder and Executive Director of Hearts at Home, an organization designed to encourage women in the profession of motherhood. Jill and her husband, Mark, have five children, four biological and one adopted. Mark is a pastor in central Illinois. Their children, Anne, Evan, Erica, Kolya, and Austin, range from ages 8 to 20.

Pam and her husband, Bill, live in Southern California with their three sons. Bill and Pam serve in full-time ministry through their speaking and writing. Bill is also a pastor. The Farrels' boys, Brock, Zach, and Caleb, range from age 14 to 21.

We live across the country from each other, but God has knit our hearts together as mothers of teenagers. We have enjoyed working together to encourage you as a mom of a teenager. Each chapter will feature a mix of our families' experiences as well as stories from many other mothers. At the end of each chapter you will find three sections that give you further encouragement:

 ### *From the Heart*

Because this is a Hearts at Home resource, Jill will share with you her thoughts on the issues addressed in the chapter. These will be straight from the heart as if you and Jill were sitting across a table, having a cup of tea together and discussing the realities of parenting teenagers.

The Next Step

We'll help you reflect and then lay out an action plan
to help you connect to your teen. By asking questions,
we'll help you formulate the next steps to take.

A Mom's Prayer
In this section, we'll offer examples of prayers you can use.
Moms know that we can't do this alone. We need wisdom
beyond our own. We need strength and the ability to love
and be courageous when our own well is dry. This section
will help you feel more comfortable with praying—talking
to God—about your teen.

In the appendix you will find discussion questions you can use with friends or in a moms' group. These will help you support and encourage one another as you forge through your children's terrific (but at times, turbulent) teen years.

When our children were toddlers, we spent a lot of time hanging out with other mothers of toddlers. As the kids have grown older, we both find ourselves with less time to hang out with women who have teenagers. We're all being stretched thin driving to and from activities and just trying to keep up with everyone's diverse schedules. That's why a resource like this is so important. It's a connection from mom to mom.

So grab a cup of tea and join us in a journey to understand the teen years. Open your heart to what God has in store for you. Enjoy the camaraderie of other moms in the trenches. We're glad you've joined us!

~Jill and Pam

A Listening Ear

Understanding and Celebrating Your Teen

As I (Jill) return home from a trip to the store, I hear music blaring from the house. I walk in to find our 17-year-old son on the computer (which doubles as a stereo), instant messaging his friends. I greet Evan (yelling over the music) and ask him to help carry in groceries. He responds with a hidden sigh and says, "Okay, Mom—just a minute. Oh, by the way, I have to work tonight—they called me in."

I head upstairs, following the distorted sounds of an electric guitar. Sticking my head in the door, I say hello to our 14-year-old daughter, Erica, who pauses strumming just long enough to say, "Hi Mom! Hey, I need my volleyball uniform washed for my game tomorrow." As I head down the hallway, the phone rings. It's our 19-year-old daughter, Anne, who is a sophomore in college. She needs to talk about her financial aid, and she asks me to look for some filed papers she needs.

That's life at the Savage home, with three teenagers and two grade schoolers to round out the family. It's noisy, busy, chaotic, high energy, scary, and fun all at the same time!

Teenagers don't come with an instruction manual—life would sure be easier if they did! The best way to learn is from others who are traveling or have traveled the journey through their children's teen years. Sometimes we need perspective, sometimes we need wisdom, and many times we just need a little bit of hope, encouragement, and reassurance from a mom who's been there. That's what Pam and I hope to bring to you as we share our lives in this book.

So let's begin by answering this question: What is a teen? A teenager is a person who...

never forgets a phone number
  but can't remember to feed the dog,
can hear a song playing three blocks away
  but not Mother calling from the next room,
can operate the latest computer without a lesson
  but can't make a bed,
has the energy to skateboard for hours
  but is too tired to mow the lawn,
will spend 12 hours studying for a driver's license test
  and 12 minutes for a history exam,
is a connoisseur of two kinds of fine music—
  loud and very loud,
is always on time for a rock concert
  but is always late for dinner,
and is sure his or her parents were never teenagers!

The Delicate Dance of Release

My (Pam) friend Debe shares a story of how the first steps of letting go were her most difficult. Her tween son, Dustin, wanted to walk down the street to hang out with some friends. She had always driven him, but he insisted she was being overprotective and that all his other junior high friends could walk a few blocks to a friend's house—even in California! She casually and calmly agreed, and her son proudly dashed out the door. When he had rounded the first corner, she dashed out the door after him like a private eye, following him and darting between bushes and behind trees so her son wouldn't see her. She knew she was being paranoid, and she didn't want her son to see her being so fearful!

Debe decided, like most moms do at some point, that she had to overcome her fears in order to give her children wings to fly. And she has done this. This same son is now a television cameraman, and his career has taken him all over the world—even into the front lines of war zones! Debe's three daughters are all very talented musicians, and they too have become world travelers. The world gets the advantage of the talent of these four children because Debe made a decision to release control incrementally regardless of how much she wanted to hang on. Having her children in the center of God's will was more important to her than having her children in the center of her living room!

Motherhood is one of the rare professions in which we actually work ourselves out of a job. A portion of our job is to care for the physical needs of our family: laundry, shopping, cooking, cleaning, organizing, mending, and any other skill that keeps a home and family working smoothly. However, during the tween and teen years, our job is to begin delegating these responsibilities to our sons and daughters. Our goal is to teach them the relational, financial, and other skills they will need to one day (we hope) fly the nest and start a career, home, and family of their own.

Releasing—it's a delicate dance. Face it, Mom—it's hard! And let's own up to this too: We sometimes don't like releasing responsibilities. Letting that junior higher out the door with friends or putting him or her on a bus to summer camp is exciting and scary! Putting that high school daughter on the arm of a young man for prom can be downright frightening. When teens take giant steps of change—when they move out to their own apartments or off to college—we are left with no bushes to hide behind to check up on their well-being! Perhaps our kids are God's tools to train us to release instead of fearfully darting back and forth behind the scenes, controlling and manipulating circumstances. At some point we have to stretch out the umbilical cord and cut it, letting our kids fly, soar, and succeed!

You Are Your Teens' Advocate Whether They Like It or Not!

My (Pam's) older two sons have both said it, and I believe it is the best and most calming statement a young adult can make: "Mom, you raised me well. Now trust the parenting job you did. I'll take all you have given me and build on it. No worries, Mom."

We do want to move to the place of "no worries" but not because we have stuck our head in the sand or because we have denied the reality of our kids' choices or behaviors. We want to confidently trust our kids, and I believe we can when we build our trust in God and see Him as our mentor. As you release, remember that God is committed to you and your child.

Mom, don't you wish you had a road map full of directions for you and your teenager? What stages will we see our tweens, teens, and college students soar through? How do we know if we are being overprotective or not protective enough? What steps can we take with our young adults so they will be adequately prepared and so that we, the moms, feel confident letting them spread their wings and fly? We don't have all the details, but we can highlight some stages and transitions most kids go through. Knowing a bit of what is on the road ahead has a calming effect on our hearts.

Hello! What's Going On in There?

Dr. Jay Giedd of the National Institute of Health has been

conducting a 13-year study into the mind of teens. He and his colleagues at UCLA, Harvard, and the Montreal Neurological Institute have discovered some interesting insights. Researchers once believed that a child's brain was nearly complete by age 12, but Dr. Giedd has discovered what all of us moms of teens have known all along—they aren't all grown-up yet! (He might have also experienced this at home—he has four teens too!) The good doctor found that the brain undergoes dramatic changes well past puberty. The medical community is looking at how brain development might impact those traits we as moms are so aware of: emotional outbursts, reckless risk taking, rule breaking, and toying with things like sex, drugs, and alcohol.

By the time a child is six years old, the brain is 90 percent of its adult size, complete with all the neurological functions. But Dr. Giedd has discovered a second wave of "proliferation and pruning that occurs later in childhood, and the final, critical part of this second wave, affecting our highest mental functions, occurs in the late teens."[1] During the teen years, the brain makes fewer but faster connections. Most scientists believe this is from "both genetics and by a use it or lose it principle." The brain seems to develop from back to front. The functions that mature earliest are in the back of the brain, including those that control interaction with the environment, such as vision, hearing, touch, and spatial processing. Next to develop are areas that help you coordinate those interactions, such as the part of the brain that helps you find the bathroom light switch in the dark because you know it's there even when you can't see it. "The very last part of the brain to be pruned and shaped to its adult dimensions is the prefrontal cortex, home of the so-called executive functions—planning, setting priorities, organizing thoughts, suppressing impulses, weighing the consequences of one's actions. In other words, the final part of the brain to grow up is the part capable of deciding, I'll finish my homework and take out the garbage, and *then* I'll IM my friends about seeing a movie."

According to UCLA neuroscientist Elizabeth Sowell, "Scientists and the general public had attributed the bad decisions teens make to hormonal changes, but once we started mapping where and when the brain changes were happening, we could say, Aha, the part of the brain that makes teenagers more responsible is not finished maturing yet."

The brain matures on a schedule, even with the onset of early or late hormonal puberty. Dr. Ronald Dahl, a psychiatrist at the University of Pittsburgh, calls this the "tinderbox of emotions" because feelings hit a flashpoint more easily, but teens also tend to seek out situations where they can allow their emotions and passions to run wild. "Adolescents are actively looking for experiences to create intense feelings. It's a very important hint that there is some particular hormone-brain relationship contributing to the appetite for thrills, strong sensations and excitement."

"The parts of the brain responsible for things like sensation-seeking are getting turned on in big ways around the time of puberty," says Temple University psychologist Laurence Steinberg, "but the parts for exercising judgment are still maturing throughout adolescence. So you've got this time gap between when things impel kids toward taking risks early in adolescence, and when things allow people to think before they act come online. It's like turning on the engine of a car without a skilled driver at the wheel."

And do you ever wonder why teens misread your emotions and say, "Don't yell at me!" or "Why are you always mad at me?" There is a reason for that too. In a series of tests at Harvard, kids and adults were both asked to identify emotions displayed in a set of photographs. "In doing these tasks, kids and young adolescents rely heavily on the amygdala, a structure in the temporal lobes associated with emotional and gut reactions. Adults, rely…more on the frontal lobe, a region associated with planning and judgment." Adults made few errors assessing the pictures, but kids under 14 tended to make more mistakes. Young teens frequently misread emotions and place anger and hostility where none exists.

And why do teens do more stupid things when they're with friends than when they're alone? Yep, science has an explanation for that too! In a driving simulator, when teens and adults were asked to make a decision to run a yellow light or not, both made wise choices when playing the game alone. Teenagers, however, took more risks when playing the game with a group of friends. Statistics show that most teen crimes occur when kids are in a gang or with friends. And it isn't just peer pressure that makes a teen vulnerable to sex, drugs, and alcohol experimentation. Rapid changes in the dopamine-rich areas of the brain make them more at risk to the addictive effects of these factors.

Why is it so hard to get your teens off the sofa to take out the trash? Their nucleus accumbens, a region in the frontal cortex that directs motivation and reward seeking—you got it—is still under development! James Bork at the National Institute on Alcoholism explains, "If adolescents have a motivational deficit, it may mean that they are prone to engaging in behaviors that have either a really high excitement factor, or a really low effort factor, or a combination of both." His suggestion to us moms is this: "When presenting suggestions, anything that parents can do to emphasize more immediate payoffs will be more effective." For example, telling your teen son that if he drinks he will be kicked off the football team is more effective than telling him he may end up on skid row.

And there is a reason you find yourself waiting up for your teens. Their melatonin levels rise slower, so their "nighttime" comes later. For years, studies have been shown that teens learn better later in the day. And they really do need more sleep as their body is changing drastically, so letting them sleep in on occasion on the weekend might make you all happier!

When is a teen's brain mature? Kids can vote and serve in the military at 18, and they are allowed to drink and gamble at 21, but they can't rent a car till age 25. The car companies might be the closest at guesstimating. Dr. Giedd says the brain reaches maturity at around age 25. He adds, "There is a debate over how much conscious control kids have. You can tell them to shape up or ship out, but making mistakes is part of how the brain optimally grows."

Tackling the Transitions

To help us navigate some of our teens' transitions, let's look at a few of their common catchphrases and what they really mean!

I Know! *(Translation: I really don't, but I want to feel in control of my world.)*

Early in the tweens, often a bit earlier for girls, adolescents go through an "I think I'm all grown-up" stage. Girls may want to wear makeup and start shaving their legs. When we (the Farrels) were youth pastors, every spring we were frustrated with eighth-grade girls. They felt they were above the rules. We had to keep going after them as they tried sneaking into the high school room, and keeping them on track in a discussion was next to impossible. They felt as if life owed them, the world should revolve around them, and the sun and moon should rise and fall at their beck and call.

This can be one of the first stressful times a mom has with her precious and formerly very helpful, kind, happy daughter. Mood swings are common just before menses begin. One mom told me, "I'll be glad when my daughter begins her period. Then at least we'll have three happy weeks a month again. Right now it is PMS 24/7!"

But girls are not the only moody ones in the house. Young men are much more sensitive right before their testosterone kicks into high gear—even prone to tears. I remember when my very emotionally stable son hit this stage. One day I asked him to do a few things around the house. When I came back more than an hour later and saw him watching TV, I pointed out that he had a list to do. He replied, "Mom, you don't have to yell. I'm a good kid, I don't do drugs or steal, and I do my homework. What do you want from me? I never seem to be good enough for you!" I had not raised my voice, and my list for him was very short for an eight-hour day, but I still witnessed a total testosterone meltdown. Emotions are raw at this stage of development.

This is also the life stage when the smart mouth, the eye rolling, and the huff and stomp kick into gear. The Farrels and Savages try to teach our children to express emotions and share feelings with respect. But tweens have a hard time knowing what disrespect looks like. Talk to your tweens and explain some code words that you will use when they cross the line into disrespect. Our (the Farrel) sons might have tried demanding and bossing us, but we'd just reply, "That was a good try. Back up and try again." In another family, the parents would say, "Circle the airport and try another landing." Early on we would give them better options for expressing their emotions.

Respect and responsibility are two keys that unlock privileges in the Farrel and Savage homes. If you do what Mom asks, or better yet, if you go above and beyond and do it with a good attitude *before* Mom asks, you are rewarded with more privileges. A track record of responsibility and success means Mom says yes much more often and offers new privileges before the kids even ask.

I Don't Want To! *(Translation: I'm afraid to.)*

"Mom, no way! Mom, you've got to be kidding! Mom, that's not fair! Mom…" Ugh, the pleasant sounds of a junior higher! Middle school is that emotionally charged limbo land where the reply to every idea is "That's stupid!"

The source of this consistently contrary attitude is fear. Tweens rarely will verbalize it, but life feels very overwhelming at this stage. They are trying to find their place in the world, and the world feels very hostile to them. They want to feel popular, well-liked, and successful in school and in social settings, but everything feels like a risk. They are faced with a huge dichotomy: *I need to find my individuality, but I don't want to stand out so far that others make fun of me.* Conformity versus individuality is the constant daily tension.

What are some ways to lower the drama and equip your middle schooler to chill out, to step out, and to sail through this stage in a successful way? Walk it through and talk it through.

Walk It Through

Before the first day of school or before any big event, walk your tween or teen through the upcoming event. One way to do this is to invite an older teen over for a meal and casually ask, "What will the first day of school be like?" or "What advice do you wish someone would have told you?" or "What should I buy or do?" By asking questions, you give your tween permission to ask questions too. And you also get information into the ears of a tween who may not have received it as well from you.

Offer to take your tween to the location of an upcoming, potentially stressful event. Some tweens will appreciate seeing the lay of the land more than others. For some, arriving five minutes early is enough to give them confidence. Offer enough time so that *you* are comfortable and can find answers to the questions your tween my have. You don't want your uneasiness to plant fear into your teen's heart. With our (the Farrels') middle son, Zach, rehearsing life established a new routine for our family and trained him to go early to events even when he could drive himself. It also trained him to call ahead and get information from coaches, leaders, or organizations. Rehearsing life helped Zach become proactive. Knowing information early helped him think through what would have been a stressful event and turn it into a successful event.

Talk It Through

During a shopping trip, over a soda, or while having a fast-food meal, ask your teen how he or she is feeling about an upcoming event or transition. Don't be discouraged if all you get is an "I dunno" or a shrug of the shoulders in response. Sometimes the question is just a way to let your tween or teen know that your door is open, and if any questions should arise in the hours or days ahead, you're available.

Sometimes talking it through means getting information into the hands of your tween: a booklet, a video, or an Internet website. Dialoging after the research is an integral step in the process, so don't shortchange your teens by just tossing a booklet their way. Offer to take them out to a favorite fast-food restaurant in a few days to talk about it.

I'м Outта Here! *(Translation: I am trying to find my path and my personhood.)*

When we were in youth work, we saw 16-year-olds hit a new phase. It coincided with them getting a driver's license. Formerly faithful youth group attenders would sometimes (not always) attend sporadically in the first few months after they got their driver's license. The sense of freedom and ownership of their life becomes the priority. Teens can be tempted to use a car to escape from things they find boring, frustrating, or confining. This is why we do not favor giving a 16-year-old keys to a new car and carte blanche to their schedule. At 16, kids do not have all the life information they need to make strategically wise choices.

Helping teens earn the right to drive more and more will ease them through this stage. Teens can drive to the store for the family, drive to and from youth group, drive siblings to their events, and run errands for you or the family in order to earn the right to use the car for fun or social events.

But cars aren't the only way teens try to escape or shut out pain or their parents. Slamming doors, isolating themselves in their room, drug and alcohol use, and premarital sex are common escapes for teens. As soon as you see signs of isolation, deal with it in a way that will open up a teen's heart. Trust your instincts. If you think your child is headed for trouble, be proactive.

I Have It Handled! *(Translation: Give me responsibility for my life in increments so I feel successful.)*

This phase usually hits just before kids' senior year or early in the fall, and by spring it's in full swing! This is a good and natural progression because young adults need to handle their own life. This stage usually manifests itself when you remind your teens of a responsibility or principle and they respond with an indignant "Mom, I have it handled!" This is sometimes accompanied by an outstretched arm which means, "Stay back, stay away, I want to do this myself." It is an older version of the toddler's cry, "Myself—do it myself!"

This can be a humorous stage. I remember one day in our son Brock's life. I asked him about some detail he needed to handle in his senior year. Brock reminded me of his responsibility track record and told me, "Don't worry, Mom! I have it handled."

Ten minutes later, Brock called. "Mom, do you think you could drive my wallet down to me at school?" Oh yeah, he had it handled!

During this stage, I asked Brock to design a signal or code so we could alert each other when we were getting on each other's nerves as he took on more responsibility. Since he was a football player, we decided that the "offsides" signal was appropriate. If I thought he was being disrespectful to me in his independence, I could throw the signal, and if he thought I was nagging him or not trusting him, he could throw it. This little bit of humor was a lifesaver the spring of his senior year. It helped us avoid the major arguments and conflicts that many of my friends were experiencing with their seniors. The best part of having a signal is that we could express a lot without having to say it, so we could use it in public or when other family members were around.

When he would throw the signal, I would say, "Okay, thanks for handling this, Brock." Sometimes I'd stop mid-sentence, knowing that if he didn't follow through, he was willing to own the issue and accept the fallout himself.

If I threw the sign, Brock would say, "Sorry Mom, I'm listening. What are you wanting to tell me?" At this point I would try, with the least amount of words, without a sarcastic tone, and without patronizing, to communicate whatever request, detail, question, or information I had for him. I tossed the ball of responsibility back into his court.

The Art of Negotiation with a Teen

To help your teens navigate their transitions and unique circumstances, you will need to have your communication skills in peak condition. And you will have to equip your teen with some basic interpersonal communication skills as well. Our tweens and teens need to learn vital communication skills, and what better way than to have us model them. Susan Alexander Yates, in her book *And Then I Had Teenagers*, explains how to resolve conflict:[2]

Conflict Resolution

Focus on...	Rather than...
one issue	many issues
the problem	the person
behavior	character
specifics	generalizations
expression of feelings	judgment of character
"I" statements	"you" statements
observation of facts	judgment of motives
mutual understanding	who's winning or losing

Before I (Pam) have a "serious talk" with one of my tweens or teens, I try to step back and think back. *Step back* means to let the heat of the moment abate before talking. *Think back* means to remember when you were their age. How did you feel? What were your fears? Your priorities?

Like Bill and Pam, Mark and I (Jill) have found that conflict is sometimes best handled away from the heat of the moment. The time to deal with getting home 30 minutes after a midnight curfew is not at 12:30 AM. The best time to deal with that is at 7:00 PM the next evening, when we can lead the conversation, stay focused on the issue at hand, and administer consequences (if needed) without the emotion of the moment.

Our teens have always responded better to discipline and accountability when we are able to address it in a respectful discussion rather than an angry, yelling conflict. I like to handle conflict swiftly and directly, so much of the time I have to exercise self-control. I want to deal with it at 12:30 AM because I need the emotional release of all that I'm feeling. However, experience has proven that sometimes the delay produces effective discussions that truly allow us to lead our teens and successfully discuss the choices they are making.

To Know

Before you have a conversation, write down the facts. Avoid reading into the facts what you think is going on or what motive might be behind your teen's choices. As the old TV show *Dragnet* says, "Just the facts, Ma'am." By wording the concern as a fact, you avoid making accusations that slam the door on conversation with teens because they feel defensive. The following examples can help you express your observations:

> Wise: "I noticed you got home at 1:00 AM."
> Unwise: "Who do you think you are, coming in at all hours!"
>
> Wise: "Honey, I've noticed you have slammed the door a lot today. Want to tell me how you are feeling?"
> Unwise: "You are not the only one who lives in this house! Have a little respect and quit slamming the door."
>
> Wise: "Here is your report card. How do you feel about your grades?"
> Unwise: "Hey, Lazybones! Do you ever study? Sure can't tell by these grades!"

Look at the "To Know" section as if you were a forensic scientist or a detective. Write down your observations: John has had headaches and stomachaches a lot this month. He's been short-tempered with me this week. He threw the bat when he struck out. He slammed the door when I asked him to clean his room. He yelled at his brother.

By stepping back and making observations, you might see patterns or other road signs that you'll miss if you jump into the conversation prematurely. The more vital the issue, the more time I spend at this stage. I pray through my child's life and ask God to help me see his or her life from a more heavenly perspective.

To Feel

This is your opportunity to put yourself in your child's shoes. As an adult, you have gradually learned how to carry more and more responsibility and pressure. But do you remember when you were pimply faced and "brace faced" too? When you were searching for your identity and that A on the paper? When sitting at a certain lunch table or having that certain someone talk to you outside science class made your day?

Do you remember the stress of a boyfriend or girlfriend giving you the cold shoulder? Or the trauma of being rejected when you asked someone to the Sadie Hawkins dance and he turned you down? Do you remember not making choir, first chair in orchestra, the cheer or dance squad? Do you remember the workload of a term paper? Perhaps now you can relate to the stress of a teen trying to make godly decisions in an ungodly world. How much energy does it take your teen to turn down cigarettes? Alcohol? Drugs? Sex?

Do you recall how hard it was to stand up for your faith when a teacher or a peer disagreed with you or was hostile toward your beliefs?

Pray and ask God to help you tune in to your tween or teen's emotional frequency. Discover what motivates your child. Every teen is a unique creation of God.

Build the Relationship

Josh McDowell, author of the book *Right from Wrong,* says "Rules without relationship equals rebellion." If you want to lower your teen's risk of rebellion, build your relationship. And one surefire way to build the relationship is to be his or her biggest fan. Be involved in your teen's world. Attend his or her games, concerts, and competitions. Volunteer to drive the van to youth group (you'll learn a lot!) and chaperone events (ask your teen first). Mark significant events and transitions in his or her life. Below are some ideas to help you celebrate your tween, teen, and young adult.

Celebrations like bar mitzvahs for Jewish boys and Quinceaneras for Hispanic girls mark the passage into the adult world. Consider the following traditions and consider how you might help your son transition into manhood or usher your daughter into her identity as a woman.

Marking Manhood

Man of Honor. Give two gifts: a sword to hang on the wall and a new Bible to remind your young man to turn to the sword of the Spirit (the Word of God) for strength as he serves the King of kings. You might include a knighting ceremony like those administered to the knights of the Round Table. This can be done at 12, 14, 16, 18, or even 21. You choose the moment of manhood you want to mark.

Draft Card Dinner. Use registering for the draft as a way to mark manhood. If your son is old enough to die for his country, he is definitely a man. Celebrate him and give a gift to help him be even more responsible, such as a briefcase, a business card holder, or his own checking account.

Walk into Manhood. Counselor Earl Henslin shared a tradition with us (the Farrels) that we have incorporated in each of our son's lives as they have headed off to college. It also can be used for eighteenth birthdays or graduation. The young man's male mentors, extended family members, adult friends, and role models (coaches, school teachers, and youth group leaders) are invited to a special celebration in honor of the 18-year-old. Dad takes the 18-year-old to a forest trail, a lakeside, a beach, or even a track. The adult male friends and family members are positioned along the route. The father and son walk the first leg together, and Dad imparts words of advice and his definition of manhood to his son. Each man takes his turn walking with the young man, imparting words of wisdom, affirmation, and perhaps a gift needed in adult life. At the trails end, all the men gather and pray over this young man as he enters adulthood.

Our oldest went off to college to play football, so we used a football field for his walk into manhood. Our middle son's mentors have relocated, so we are planning a drive into manhood. He will drive from mentor to mentor's home, and they will offer their words of wisdom to him over a meal. His dad will accompany him and use the driving time to offer advice. Each mentor brings a quote or a Bible verse to go in a scrapbook along with his picture, address, and phone number.

Shaving Rituals. Giving a tween or early teen all the goods for shaving when his voice begins to change is a nice touch. It can be accompanied with a meal out with "the men" where everyone can share a story beginning with "I knew I was a man when..."

A Celebration of Womanhood

Here are a few ways to celebrate your daughter and her step across the threshold into womanhood:

The Beginning. Beginning menses can be a traumatic experience. But a mother can turn trauma into triumph with a little tender loving care. When your daughter begins menstruation, let her play hooky from school for a day. Take her to get her first grown-up silky nightgown, let her try on a precious set of pearls, or have her makeup done at the department store makeup counter. If letting her take a day off school doesn't fit your style, then plan a girls' night out at a fancy café. Present her with a dozen roses and maybe a delicate charm bracelet that you can add to with every future big moment in her teen life. Somehow, someway, celebrate her beginning moment as a true woman.

Terrific Twelve. You might be able to beat your daughter to the starting line of womanhood by making her twelfth birthday packed with firsts. (For some early bloomers, you might need to move this up a year, and do a "Heavenly Eleven" party.) Buy her first razor to shave her legs, her first set of high heels, or her first makeup set. Let her get her ears pierced or take the next age-appropriate step.

For your daughter's sixteenth birthday (or whenever you feel she is ready to date), try one of these ideas:

On the Town. Host a formal dinner party where her closest friends (guys and gals) dress to the nines and eat the fanciest gourmet food you can afford. Play classical music, or hire a harpist or a string quartet.

Dance the Night Away. Host a dance where couples learn some ballroom steps, like the waltz, swing, tango, and two-step. You will have to spring for a DJ, dance instructor, and food, but the evening will definitely create some wonderful memories.

High Tea. Take her and a few of her closest friends (and maybe their moms or all the female relatives) to high tea. Bring along photos of her growing-up years—and yours. Hand down a piece of jewelry that has been in the family for a couple generations.

Passport 2 Purity. As she enters her teen years, take her away for a special weekend with mom. Using Family Life's Passport 2 Purity resource pack, discuss her changing body and the new season of life she is entering.[3] Take some time to go shopping and have some special girl time to mark this transition in her life. (Passport 2 Purity can also be used with your teen son.)

Terrific 21 for a Son or Daughter

Your family can demonstrate that drinking and gambling are not the best ways to celebrate this milestone. I (Pam) had a quilt made from all the "award" T-shirts Brock had earned in high school and college. It was pre-tied so that the strings were pulled through, but friends and family gathered to pray for him and tie the knots.

You might take a trip to test his or her toughness or bring a dream into reality: white-water rafting, parachuting, mountain climbing, or bicycling across the country or across Europe. If the fear factor is an issue for you, contract the trip with trained professionals.

One mother hid gifts around a mall and left a trail of clues. Each gift stood for a positive quality in her daughter's life. You can also give some much needed R and R: a trip to a special place, such as a day spa, a mountain cabin, or a houseboat. Or you can be practical and give your 21-year-old a leg up in the world with a car or a house or condo down payment. For a more realistic budget, consider a briefcase, a business outfit or suit, or spend as little as $7 for some business cards.

 ### *From the Heart*

I remember many things about my tumultuous teen years, but I remember more activities and events than emotions. The teen years are a jumble of emotions as the brain and the rest of the body are maturing at different rates of speed.

My memories from junior high and high school can serve me well as a mom if I'll allow them to. An occasional story from the "olden days" is valuable to a parent-teen relationship, but even more important is the ability to empathize with what our teen is feeling. When I can operate with empathy, I am empowered with grace and patience that go a long way in ushering my child into adulthood.

When I think hard about the emotions I experienced in high school, I can dredge up feelings like fear, rejection, pressure, excitement, hope, and joy. I remember feeling empowered one minute and incredibly naive the next. When I can remember and do my best at relating to my teens, I find that empathy makes me a much more patient, kind, and gentle mom. When I can recognize the emotional roller coaster they are on, I am less likely to take their words and actions as personal offenses against me. This allows for objectivity and sets us up for a far more enjoyable ride through the teen years.

The Next Step

Look at the next big step in your teenagers' lives and plans. How can you celebrate them and their ability to make wise decisions at this next juncture in life?

A Mom's Prayer

Lord, as I journey through this book and my child's teen years, give me wisdom and hope. Remind me often that I was once a teen and have become a responsible adult, so You can pull my teen through to success too! Amen.

Casting Vision

Helping Your Teens Find Their Path

"I want to be a fireman."

"I want to be an actress."

"I want to be president."

When kids are toddlers, their hoping and wishing is fun. But as they enter junior high, more weighs on their decisions, so helping them find their niche becomes more important—and complicated. From our years of working with teenagers in the school system (Jill) and in the church (Pam), we have found that those students who had a good sense of self, who discovered their talents, skills, and gifts, seemed to sail through their teen years. A tween who feels good about something he or she can do is less likely to be swayed by negative peer pressure. Instead of being led astray by others, those who have a platform they can stand on become the leaders.

Pursuing Their Purpose

Some tweens and teens have skills and gifts that are easy to pinpoint, like sports, scholastic achievement, or music. But other abilities are less apparent: starting and running a business, teaching children, cooking and other home skills, or hunting and fishing. Some students' strengths are less obvious than others. They may be caring, kind, funny, and hard-working; they may have high morals, love for God, and servant's hearts—just the kind of talents that make for a very successful pastor, missionary, or white-collar professional. However, being good with people isn't a skill set that is easily rewarded in high school, so the adults in these students' lives need to send compliments and encouragement their way.

Give a Compliment

One way is to compliment character. Try to find creative ways to applaud those less noticeable but vital gifts and skills. One mom I met was concerned that her junior higher (who had a learning disability) might get discouraged at report card time, so she gave a character report card. She gave grades in things like kindness, helpfulness, hard work, and generosity.

Another way to open up options to your children, especially ones who may struggle academically, is to compliment adults you interact with who do their jobs especially well. Send a thank-you letter to the sales person or hotel clerk who went out of her way to help you. Read the letter to your child before you send it. Thank the nurse, X-ray technician, and admitting staff after hospital visits—not just the doctor. Ask your child to help you select a small gift for your postal worker, mechanic, or hairdresser. Thank every military person, law enforcement officer, and firefighter you meet. As you respect people in a variety of fields, more opportunities open in your child's mind. Invest in some lessons or some summer camps, or create an internship by finding a way for your child to volunteer or shadow a professional. Many service fields provide a very good living, and in a constantly changing world, the career your child might choose may not even be invented yet!

In Your Own Backyard

Check local parenting magazines that are often found sitting next to library checkout stations, at grocery stores, or at gyms. They will often list local groups sponsoring activities, camps, and conferences aimed at enhancing young lives. Some of the activities may even be free: local art museums, science museums, and zoos may sponsor special days at reduced or no fees.

In Your Own Friendship Circle

Perhaps you have a friend who shares the same interest as one of your children: scrap booking, mechanics, model building, or cooking. One of my (Pam's) dear friends discovered when teaching my son's junior high home economics class that Zach loved to cook. She gave him a few cooking supplies for a birthday gift, and another friend, a gourmet caterer, sent a cookbook Zach's way. Zach decided in high school to take a more advanced cooking class. Zach is popular among his college friends because he cooks for them! (And I am hopeful that one day his future wife will thank my friends for nurturing a young man who both cooks and does the dishes!)

On the Road Ahead

Some opportunities might come from a student just older than your own. Maybe a neighbor, friend, or older student would be willing to mentor or hang out with your student. You might know someone who is great with computers or would give batting lessons or music lessons. My son took some art lessons from a college student who was grateful for the extra money.

On the Internet

The Web is a great resource to discover camps and conferences, but you'll need to thoroughly check out any of these opportunities because pedophiles know children gravitate toward enriching opportunities. Look for reputable organizations that offer endorsements and have been in business a long time. The best recommendation is from someone you know who had a positive experience.

In Your Network

Your children's teachers, coaches, and school counselors can track down opportunities to enrich your children. Those in the field you are looking to develop always know the best and most respected leaders, camps, conferences, clubs, and classes in that field.

Who Are They in the Forest of Life?

While on a speaking team with Kay Warren at Saddleback Church, I had the good fortune of hearing Kay explain a brilliant, easy-to-use grid for assessing personality traits. You might be familiar with Hippocrates' four basic temperaments: sanguine, choleric, melancholic, and phlegmatic—not words you use every day, nor are they easy to spell! Or perhaps you have taken the DISC test, which describes the temperaments on four variables: dominance, influence, steadiness, and conscientiousness. John Trent and Gary Smalley explain the personalities with animals in their books *The Two Sides of Love* and *The Treasure Tree*. The lion is the natural leader, the otter is the playful people person, the beaver is the hardworking detail-oriented personality, and the retriever is the loyal and easygoing person. Kay described the personalities in a much easier and more familiar way. If you are familiar with Winnie the Pooh, her framework is easier to use. I have listed her names and added our own explanation of each personality, ideas for motivating each personality, and a key word to remember that personality. Do any of these descriptions fit your teen?

Winnie the Pooh (phlegmatic, retriever, steady)

Key word: peaceful

Motivator: respect

Strengths: low-key, calm, cool, patient, quiet, sympathetic, witty, agreeable, steady, dependable, finds the easier solution, pleasant, listener, compassionate

Weaknesses: fearful, indecisive, avoids responsibility, shy, not goal-oriented or self-motivated, lazy, careless, uninvolved, unexcitable, judgmental, sarcastic, hates change

Everybody loves this happy-go-lucky Pooh Bear. They are people-oriented, easy-going, and loyal friends. Not much rocks their world. Everyone gets along with Pooh Bear even when they can't get long with each other. Winnie has an inborn mediator talent.

Even though they have an easygoing nature, these children might be the hardest to motivate because they desire acceptance and respect. They long to be loved and valued not for what they can do but rather who they are. Typical chore charts and stars and bars don't work all that well with these teens. They don't want to be defined by their accomplishments or the hoops they jump (or more likely—refuse to jump) through.

Tigger (sanguine, otter, influential)

Key word: people

Motivator: attention

Strengths: talkative, outgoing, enthusiastic, sincere, positive, spontaneous, adventurous, inspirational, charming, friendly, forgiving, fun, popular

Weaknesses: Talkative, exaggerates, wears rose-colored glasses, naive, lives by circumstances, forgetful, undisciplined, distracted, needs approval of friends too much, fickle, excuse maker

This creature defines him or herself as "bouncy, trouncy, flouncy, pouncy, fun, fun, fun, fun, fun." These people are also people oriented with a high need for fun! They are a party waiting to happen. You can get people with this personality to do anything if you can convince them it is fun.

Eeyore (melancholy, conscientious, beaver)

Key word: perfect

Motivator: answers and structure

Strengths: analytical, creative, deep, sacrificial, conscientious, organized, economical, behind-the-scenes servant, idealistic

Weaknesses: negative, moody, introspective, can avoid people, hard to please, critical, withdrawn, socially awkward, unforgiving, skeptical, reserved, unaffectionate

Eeyore is famous for his line, "It'll never work." Eeyores tend to see the glass half empty. These folks see life at a deeper level. They make awesome artists and musicians. However, because they see life deeper, they can be prone to depression. My husband, Bill, says they are "evidence gatherers." If they are on a healthy track emotionally, they have gathered evidence of God's goodness and tapped into the positive side of people and life. However, if they get off track, they gather evidence that life is the pits, and you'll hear them say things like "Life stinks." They will get depressed and stay depressed. They are prone to self-mutilation and suicide. They can spiral themselves downward.

One way to handle this predisposition toward the negative is to help them create a bottom, a place where they can launch themselves upward. For example, Bill taught one young man to "stop, drop, and roll." When he realized he was being negative, he was to say "Stop!" aloud—a kind of wake-up call for change. Then he was to drop to his knees to pray and ask God for help. And finally, he was to roll over and do some preset activities: a walk around the block, a call to a friend, or some other positive activity to change the setting.

To motivate these people, give them answers. Here's the plan; this is why we are doing it that way. As they get older, you can ask them to create the plan or structure. Be careful making promises to this teen. For example, if you say, "Tomorrow we'll go shopping," and you don't go, you didn't just "get busy." No, you lied!

Owl (choleric, lion, dominant)

> *Key word:* power
>
> *Motivator:* control
>
> *Strengths:* leader, active, change agent, strong willed, goal oriented, self-motivated, confident, overcomer, great under pressure
>
> *Weaknesses:* low need for friends, bossy, brassy, quick-tempered, non-emotional, workaholic, ends justify the means, know-it-all, too independent

In the adventures of Winnie the Pooh, Owl was the wise leader, the mentor-like friend who helped Pooh get a grip and get a plan. This is probably the easiest personality to spot because Owls may proclaim themselves the leader, or you might see their friends always look to them to make decisions. They tend to be firstborns but not always. They are task oriented and can get the job done.

To motivate these teens, give them some control over their life. Give them choices, options, and the opportunity to create the path. They are natural leaders, so give them chances to lead. If you try to make all their decisions, these strong-willed teens will make your life one big long power struggle.

At times, you will have to show Owls that you are "tough enough to take them." This just means that you may have to outlast them or outwit them. My husband gave our strong-willed son, who bench-presses more than 300 pounds, this teasing reminder: "Son, you might think you are strong enough to take me, but I can starve you out." It was a gentle but profound way to remind him that his parents are wiser, and they hold the checkbook and car keys.

Unwrap the Gift

God gives people spiritual gifts, which the Bible explains are for the "building up of the body." In other words, they are not for self-gratification but for making the world a better place. One way to discern a spiritual gift is to have your teen take a spiritual gift inventory like the one found at www.elmertowns.com. (Under "Resources," select "Spiritual Gifts Questionnaire.")

The best way to discover spiritual gifts is to try using them! Each August, we ask our children how they will serve God, the church, and Christian organizations in the upcoming school year. We help them see needs in the organizations and in the community, and we talk about how their gifts might help meet those needs.

To help teens understand their gifts, talents, and skills, and to help them use those strengths in their own unique way, have them complete this journaling exercise: On a sheet of paper, write five to seven sentences or short paragraphs that describe times in your life you have volunteered, helped other people, or given of yourself in some way that either you enjoyed or people complimented you for. Then go back and look for common phrases, repeated words, or themes. What stood out to you from this exercise?

By looking for repeating patterns, teens can discern God's fingerprints and anointing on their lives.

When the Experiment Goes Awry

Teens begin defining themselves by their group, such as cheerleaders, skaters, musicians, and athletes. They like to try on their different identities and roles. Some fit, some don't. For a mother, this can be a scary series of events. We see our child dress or act differently—sometimes very differently! We need a way to know which hills to die on, which issues are nonnegotiable. Every issue can't be the defining issue, so as your child experiments with his or her identity, try to keep a few principles in mind. Know when to draw the line.

Knowing when to draw the line, when to let kids figure out who they are and experiment, is sometimes a tough thing. To the Farrel family, the line came down to a few very key principles based on a couple valuable Scripture verses. Ask these questions to know when to draw the L.I.N.E.:

Lifestyle

Is this action, attitude, or decision going to help build long-term, healthy patterns into his or her life? For example, bulimia and anorexia might be effective ways to temporarily lose weight, but in the long run they are fatal.

Ask yourself, *Is this permanent or temporary?* If it can grow back or grow out, don't freak out. Buzzed hair, a Mohawk, or pink or blue hair is all very unnerving, but it is temporary. Susan Alexander Yates says this in *And Then I Had Teenagers:*

> Separate swing issues from crucial issues…Crucial issues are these issues that have to do with character: integrity, compassion, responsibility, respect, self-discipline. Crucial issues are those on which the Bible has clear teaching: sex outside marriage, murder, stealing. Our laws would also constitute crucial issues…Swing issues on the other hand, aren't always so cut and dried. It isn't clear how to handle them. Trendy dress, earrings, belly rings, blue hair, tattoos, messy rooms…There are no easy answers, but there are some guidelines…What do we do when issues seem to cross the grey line from swing to crucial?…We have to define the line.[1]

If it isn't immoral or illegal, hear their case. You will need to say no to many things: no drugs, no drinking, no premarital sex, no skipping class. If you can, say, "I'll think about it" or "Tell me why I should say yes." Making a case for a privilege is good for a teen.

In the Savage home, our daughter Anne really wanted a nose stud. Several girls in her class were getting them, and she asked off and on for two years. When we began to ask her about her career goal of being an elementary teacher and how a nose piercing might affect her ability to secure a job, her perspective began to change.

In the same way, our teenage son, Evan, asked to get his ears pierced for more than three years. When he was approaching his sixteenth birthday, we heard him out and asked him the same questions we had asked his sister. Evan's career goal is to be a studio musician and work in the recording industry. In his case, pierced ears wouldn't be as big of a deal and most likely wouldn't affect his ability to be hired into any job in the industry.

Identity

Will this decision build my family's reputation? My team's? My club's? Teens have a difficult time with this. They may say "It's not hurting anyone," or "It's my life!" But we are all tied together. Your life impacts my life, and my life impacts yours. Some teens struggle with the fishbowl more than others. The children of politicians, pastors, doctors, lawyers, and police or military officers are held to a higher standard. They might not appreciate the double standard, but these teens' lives do impact their families. This can either be seen as an advantage or disadvantage. We (the Farrels) chose to help our children see it as an advantage. The high degree of accountability helps them make wise choices. All kids should have this advantage.

When you help your teens find their dream, you give them something to live for. When you help them see that their life matters in God's plan, they have a better reason to say no to negatives and distractions and yes to cooperation with God, to you, and to organizations and institutions that will build their future.

Nonsense

Sometimes the answers are just obvious. "Duh." Here are a few answers I've heard moms give to questions that kids shouldn't even bother asking:

- No, you can't walk across town alone through a crime-ridden neighborhood just so you can buy lip gloss.
- No, you cannot practice driving. You're only 12, and I don't care if we do live in a cul-de-sac.

- No, you can't use shoe cleaner to start the fire in the fire-place. No, you can't squeeze gasoline onto it either.

- No, you may not go on a date. You're 12 and he's 21.

If your teens will harm themselves or others, the answer is no!

Evangelism

This is just a 50-cent word for representing God as an ambassador. Have your teens ask themselves, *Will my dress, actions, and words communicate who Christ is?* Explain that we are all ambassadors. When tweens and teens understand that they might be someone's only light of truth, they catch how important, vital, and needed they are. Plan experiences into your teens' lives that will give them a glimpse of just how important God thinks they are.

One mom had a teen daughter with a bad attitude. She was bucking the family at every turn. She didn't want to wear what her parents wanted her to wear, she didn't want to do or be anything her parents suggested. They went to the Lord, and on their knees in prayer, intervened on behalf of their daughter. Their church's youth group was taking a six-week missions trip to the barrios of Mexico. The parents knew it would get their daughter out of her downward spiral, away from friends who also had bad attitudes and were making bad choices. It would take a miracle to get their daughter to want to go. So they prayed, and their strong-willed daughter came home announcing she *wanted* to go on this missions trip.

On the trip, God got ahold of her heart. She realized how very fortunate she was in contrast to the poverty and illiteracy she saw. Priorities shifted as she served others and saw lives changed because she was there. She came home with a desire to win her campus for Christ and to later attend a Christian university so she could become a leader who could impact her generation. While on the trip, she had to follow a dress code that enforced modesty in order to maintain credibility. When she returned home, she no longer had a mandatory dress code, but God had adjusted her heart, and she now desired more modest attire. More than anything, she saw that her parents were wise and on her side; they were not her enemies but her advocates. She began to seek out their advice. The best part is that this experience preached the lesson so they didn't have to! Look for experiences that help your teens see that God can use their life. When they see how exciting life is when they serve God, God has their attention, and the Holy Spirit can gently whisper what you tried screaming and shouting.

What Is God's Will, Anyway?

There are many built-in opportunities to help your tween, teen, and college students learn to discern the will of God in their life: which activity to choose, when to get an after-school job and where, whom to date (or later, whom to marry), what classes to take, what to major in, and where to attend college. With so many questions, teens must learn how to hear from God on their own because, like it or not, you won't be around forever! Three *C*'s can help your family discern God's heart.

Counsel

The best source of knowing the will of God is the Word of God. Psalm 37:4 says, "Delight yourself in the LORD and he will give you the desires of your heart." An amazing thing happens when you read the Bible. Your heart and your desires change. Reading the Bible transforms your will, and you begin to want what God wants. So when you read His Word and then request something from God, He is more likely to say yes.

Another way to get good counsel is to rally a set of advisors who know you and love you, and who know God and love God's Word. Proverbs 11:14 says, "For lack of guidance a nation falls, but many advisers make victory sure." Encourage your son or daughter to have mentors and close relationships with youth workers, pastors, and other Christian leaders. Your teens will see that the adults in their life care and are concerned for them. When decision-making time comes around, your teens will automatically and naturally seek out the advice of those role models. No one knows God's will better than the individual whom God is leading, but often students will see a pattern as they talk through the issue or decision with their sounding board.

Confirming Information

Many resources specialize in career and scholastic development to help young people discover their niche. One of the best resources the Farrels used was the LifePathways software from Crown Financial Ministries. This software (or the online test) surveys your student in a variety of areas, including skills, interests, values, and personality. This comprehensive test then prints a personalized path or set of options in your student's area of study. It suggests majors and careers based on the answers given. When our two older sons took the test (the summer after their junior year), the results confirmed the direction we already believed God had given. We had an idea of things we thought our sons would be good at and enjoy, and the survey confirmed what we thought in our heart and made specific recommendations on majors and career options.

As you gather information from many different sources, the multitude of options will funnel into a final choice that will emerge as the best field for your son or daughter.

Conviction of the Holy Spirit

Romans 8:16 says God's Spirit testifies with our spirit. Sometimes we know that we know that we know that God is guiding us toward a decision. He often repeats Himself to get our attention. Our conversations, the things we read, and our circumstances sometimes confirm the direction He's leading us.

Teach your teen that peace comes only as you step out into God's will. God often doesn't part the waters until you step out. The people of Israel couldn't cross the Jordan until their leaders stepped out into the water—so encourage your teen to step out by faith and trust that God will meet him or her.

When the Going Gets Tough

Somewhere along the path your sons or daughters may lose motivation or feel discouraged. How can you help them pick themselves up, dust themselves off, and start all over again?

Sometimes we need to remind ourselves of God's promises for our kids before we can remind our kids: God will be with them. He will make a path for them. He loves them even more than we do, and He longs to be good to them!

> And therefore the Lord [earnestly] waits [expecting, looking, and longing] to be gracious to you; and therefore He lifts Himself up, that He may have mercy on you and show loving-kindness to you. For the Lord is a God of justice. Blessed (happy, fortunate, to be envied) are all those who [earnestly] wait for Him, who expect and look and long for Him [for His victory, for His favor, His love, His peace, His joy, and His matchless, unbroken companionship]! (Isaiah 30:18 AMP).

 ### *From the Heart*

While I was writing my portions of this chapter, our oldest daughter, Anne, made a very difficult decision to leave the private

Christian college she was attending and transfer to a less expensive state school to finish her teaching degree. It was a heart-wrenching decision for her and a heart-wrenching experience for us to watch her seek God and struggle to make the decision.

As Anne was making this decision, I found myself being the vision caster in our discussions. I tried to present many different perspectives and help her consider how her decision today will affect her future.

The hardest part was watching her make the decision on her own. My prayers during this season have been for her to sense clear direction from God and for me to know my role in letting go, casting vision, and giving leadership.

During our children's teen years, our role changes from decision maker to vision caster as we help them make their own decisions for their life.

The Next Step

Proverbs 18:16 says, "A man's gift makes room for him and brings him before great men." Florence Litteaur says, "If you do what you do better than anyone else, you will always be a success." Consider the ways students can discover who they are and how to best use their skills, talents, and gifts. What activity (or activities) would you like to schedule to help your tween or teen find his or her own path?

A Mom's Prayer

Lord, help me see my teen through Your eyes. Help me not focus on the problems but see the potential in my son or daughter. Make his or her future path clear. Amen.

On Being a Mentor

Equipping a Teen with People Skills and Life Skills

The doorbell rang, and our youngest ran to the door to answer it. It was a woman from the church who was dropping something off for my husband. As I (Jill) walked from the far end of the house to greet her, she was entering our kitchen. One of our teens sat at the family computer in the kitchen, instant messaging his friends. Another sat at the kitchen island, thumbing through a magazine that had just arrived in the mail. Neither spoke to our guest in the kitchen. After our guest's visit, I realized that I had a hospitality lesson to teach.

Moms have the opportunity to teach homemaking and hospitality skills that teenagers need to learn. These will equip our young adults with the people skills and the home-management skills they will need as employees, neighbors, coworkers, church members, husbands or wives, and friends who care.

Our children are not born knowing how to extend hospitality to those around them. They don't automatically know how to care for their home. Their first lessons come from watching how we handle relationships and personal belongings. Certainly more is caught than taught, but moms need to share additional lessons. Just look at what you learned from your mother:

_____

Things My Mother Taught Me

My mother taught me logic: "Because I said so, that's why."

My mother taught me medicine: "If you don't stop crossing your eyes, they're going to freeze that way."

My mother taught me humor: "When that lawn mower cuts off your toes, don't come running to me."

My mother taught me about genetics: "You're just like your father!"

My mother taught me about my roots: "Do you think you were born in a barn?"

My mother taught me about anticipation: "Just wait until your father gets home."

My mother taught me to appreciate a job well done: "If you're going to kill each other, do it outside—I just finished cleaning!"

My mother taught me religion: "You better pray that will come out of the carpet."

My mother taught me foresight: "Wear clean underwear—you might get in an accident."

My mother taught me irony: "Keep laughing and I'll *give* you something to cry about."

My mother taught me about the science of osmosis: "Shut your mouth and eat your supper!"

My mother taught me about contortionism: "Will you *look* at the dirt on the back of your neck!"

My mother taught me about hypocrisy: "If I've told you once, I've told you a million times—don't exaggerate!"

My mother taught me about envy: "Millions of less fortunate children in this world don't have wonderful parents like you do!"

And my mother taught me about justice: "One day you'll have kids, and I hope they turn out just like *you*. Then you'll see what being a parent is like."

Seriously, we learn some of the most practical things from our mothers: how to boil water, wash our clothes, pay our bills, and mind our manners! This chapter is packed with practical things you can teach your teens.

Hospitality

After our guest went on her way, I shared with the kids that having people in our home is an opportunity to impart value to them. It's a chance to touch someone's heart. It's an occasion to make people feel welcome in a place that's not their own. Then I went on to explain to them the importance of greeting and speaking to a guest in our home. If they don't know the person, they should introduce themselves with a handshake and the words, "Hi, I don't believe I've had the opportunity to meet you. I'm _____." If they know the person, they need to stop what they are doing and acknowledge the guest's presence. A simple greeting of "Hello, _____. How are you?" is appropriate. After a greeting and introduction, if necessary, they can certainly return to whatever they were doing. The next time the doorbell rang, our guest was greeted much differently!

I (Pam) remember when my own mother taught us how to greet guests. Before opening the door to greet a guest, she shut off the television. All three of us kids said, "Aw, Mom!" to which she calmly replied, "We want guests in our home to know they are more important to us than any actor we *don't even know!*"

Introductions

Before our "greeting our guest" lesson on hospitality, we (the Savages) had had a similar lesson on handling introductions. A family wedding was approaching, and Mark and I knew that the kids would be meeting friends and relatives they'd never met before. We also knew they really hadn't been shown how to handle introductions appropriately.

With just a few intentional minutes, we gave them some simple instructions about handling an introduction: Look the person in the eye, extend a firm handshake, and respond with "It's nice to meet you." At the wedding, we introduced our children to dozens of people they'd never met, and the kids responded appropriately because they had been given the tools to do so. On the way home, our 13-year-old daughter said, "Mom, thanks for telling us how to meet someone. I've never met so many new people in my life!"

Manners

Table manners are important life skills that children need to know. Each mom will have her own way of teaching these skills. One mom I know plans one evening meal each month served with her best china, cloth napkins, multiple utensils (What do you do with two forks and two spoons?), and candlelight. She uses this as a time to talk about table etiquette, such as placing the napkin on your lap, using the silverware from the outside to the inside, learning to ask for something to be passed rather than reaching for it, and using a butter knife to place the butter on your plate before using your own knife to spread it on your bread.

Other friends of ours take their children out to eat once a month at a nice restaurant to give them the same instructions and opportunities to learn. When they eat dinner together as a family each evening at home, they reinforce those lessons. When our own kids were teens, our youth group held at least one event a year that was formal so the teens could experience a formal dinner in an emotionally safe environment.

It is so easy to be afraid of making a social blunder. Here are a few things that will help your teen get it right:

- It's always right to help others feel more comfortable. Someone else at the party or at the table is probably feeling scared or uncomfortable too. Focus on helping them feel at home or at ease. That's why someone with manners will never point out others' failures of manners in a public setting. People matter more than rules.

- It's always right to be appreciative and thankful, not critical. Teach your tween and teen that no one owes them anything. Every kindness should be appreciated.

- It's right to work from the outside in at any formal dinner setting.

- It's always right to smile, show compassion, and say "Thank you," "Can I help?" "Can I offer you something to drink?" "Please," and "I am sorry, please forgive me."

- It's always right to say positive things, and if you can't say something nice, don't say anything at all—or change the topic! It's always appropriate to move a negative conversation toward something more positive. This doesn't mean we avoid controversy, but we teach our children to avoid criticism, gossip, and unproductive conversations.

- It's always right to talk things out ahead of time if money is involved. Having a plan for shared finances, house rules, and traditions will help everyone feel more relaxed and avoid misunderstandings.

- It's always right to introduce others: older to younger, women to men, higher ranking to lower. It's always nice to add a compliment to the introductions as well as some kind of connection to you, to something they both enjoy, or to a topic they might enjoy talking about.

- It's always right to introduce yourself, and it's always right to help someone look good. If you aren't introduced in the first few seconds, someone may have forgotten your name. Help them out by introducing yourself and sharing how you know the host or the person you thought might introduce you. Offer a handshake.

- It's always right to think of others. Turn off your cell phone (or put it on manners mode). Return calls *after* you spend time with the person you are with. When leaving a message, give all the vitals: who, what, when they can call and catch you, and your phone number.

- It's always right to be on time, to be prepared, and to help out. (The fastest way to make a forever friend or good impression is to help clean up at the end of an event!)

- It's always right to be grateful. If you are a guest, bring a little gift: flowers, a plant, some chocolates...and always send a thank-you afterward. When receiving a gift, thank the giver in person, and send a handwritten thank-you note too.

- It's always right to be a good listener. When people say, "She is a great conversationalist," what they usually mean is that she is good at asking a question and then listening!

- It's always right to stand when someone is introduced to you, to stand and offer your seat to someone older, or to stand and help someone whose arms are full. And it's always right to "stand up" for the needy, the downtrodden, and the bullied.

Chivalry Isn't Dead

The feminism movement has left many of our men and boys confused about how to show respect to women and girls. I (Jill) believe that chivalry is not dead, and we can model and teach it to our sons.

I would be the first to admit that I do not have the same physical strength as a man. When lugging around a 50-pound suitcase on a trip, I am more than happy when a man says, "May I help you with that?" I appreciate a man who recognizes that he has a gift to give and shares it readily!

Our sons need to know that they help a woman feel valuable when they open a car door for her. They show respect when they give up their seat for a lady. They bestow honor when they step ahead and open the door to a building. And offering to carry in the groceries for mom is an act of kindness and strength that prepares our sons to be a blessing to their wives.

One of my favorite movies is *Kate and Leopold*. It's a wonderful romance between a woman from today's culture who, through a rip in time, falls in love with a man from the 1800s. Leopold's old-fashioned manners, respect for women, chivalry, and general acts of courtesy win the heart of Kate, who is far more accustomed to dating men who have a me-first and get-what-you-can attitude. Leopold's actions show her that she is beautiful and valuable. He speaks volumes with his simple courtesies.

What may be now labeled as old-fashioned is simply the lost art of showing respect and courtesy. It's an art that our sons need to know and be encouraged to embrace. In the same way, our daughters need to learn how to be encouraging and respectful to young men who try to show these gestures of grace and kindness. Guys risk when they step out to open a door, pull out a chair, or help with boxes or baggage. A young woman who smiles and gives a thank-you helps encourage a young man to continue to be kind.

Homemaking

I recently had a phone conversation with our oldest daughter, Anne, who is a sophomore in college. I asked what she had been doing that week, and she responded that she seemed to be spending a lot of time teaching the freshman girls how to do laundry. "Mom, I'm amazed at how many girls have never done a load of laundry!"

When our children were small, we assigned daily "family responsibilities." I personally don't like the word *chore* because it has a negative connotation and doesn't adequately describe the nature of the tasks that we need to do on a regular basis. Those everyday responsibilities are what we do behind the scenes to help our lives run smoothly. They are the tasks our family takes for granted until Mom is incapacitated in some way and can't keep up with the work or she intentionally passes responsibilities on to her children as they become old enough to handle them.

We're really not doing our children a favor by handling all of these responsibilities until they leave home. A teacher doesn't do the work for her students. Instead she teaches them how to do the work, works alongside them, and then allows them to fly on their own. We need to teach our children how to handle the around-the-house skills they will need once they are in a college dorm room, in an apartment on their own, or in their own home with their own family.

Laundry

If they wear the clothes, they can help wash the clothes—that's the mantra in the Savage home. From the time our kids were preschoolers and were beginning to identify their colors, they were helping me sort laundry. If you didn't start early in your home, it's never too late to start with tweens and teens. Teach them the process from sorting the clothes to measuring the detergent to cleaning the dryer filter. Make sure that they understand that the task isn't finished until the clean clothes are put away in their drawers.

One mom I know requires her children in seventh grade and older to do their own laundry. She spends one Saturday in August teaching them how to do the laundry, including hand washing and air-drying delicate items. After that lesson day, the laundry responsibility is theirs. If they want that special shirt to wear to a ball game, they need to plan ahead and make sure it's clean!

At the Savage home, laundry is everyone's responsibility. We don't require our kids to do their own laundry, but we expect them to help when asked and to pitch in without asking. We've taken the time to state that expectation formally as they've entered upper grade school and junior high. In the Farrel home, each son has a "rite of passage" in fifth grade. We give them money to select their own school clothes and then teach them how to do their own laundry. From that point on, they are in charge of their own wardrobe and wardrobe care.

Whatever way you decide to teach your children how to do laundry, the most important thing to do is to teach them and equip them with the knowledge and experience to do the job when they are out on their own. When they begin driving, they can even take over the family's dry cleaning runs!

Cleaning

When I (Jill) was a freshman in high school, I held my first job. I spent my Saturdays cleaning the house of a woman in our church. Florence was a widow of many years and had carried the full responsibility of home and family for a long time. She was a very independent woman who not only ran a printing business in an office behind her large farmhouse but also raised sheep and played semiprofessional tennis.

Florence was an expert delegator, and she invested in the lives of young people like me. Two or three girls worked in the house, and several high school boys worked in the barn and did the yard work on Saturdays. Some of us doubled as employees of her printing business, and I occasionally cared for her handicapped daughter, fed the sheep, or mowed the yard.

Florence was an excellent teacher. Whenever I did a new job for her, she always took the time to teach me how to do it. She never threw me into a responsibility without helping me understand both why and how a job was to be done. I always felt equipped to do whatever she asked me to do. To this day, I clean my house the way Florence taught me to clean.

I've passed on the wisdom and processes I learned from Florence to my children. We can't expect our children to know how to clean— we need to teach them. During their third- and fourth-grade years, I work alongside them when cleaning their room, changing their sheets, and sorting through their stuff. Just as Florence showed me how to do the job, I take this season to show the kids how to clean and organize, giving them just a little more responsibility of their own each time we work together. From the time they enter fifth grade, we expect our kids to clean their own room and change the sheets on their own bed once a week.

Both boys and girls need to know how to care for their home and their belongings. They need to understand that the home they want to bring their friends to needs to be cared for and maintained. However, they need to be taught how to do the job, mentored along the way, and then empowered to carry the responsibility on their own.

Organization

Pam and I both confess: We are messy at heart. I have to think hard about organizing things, and I have to intentionally work to put things away instead of piling them up. My children tend to be the same way. When children are preschoolers and grade-schoolers, Mom usually keeps papers and personal items organized (and some of us struggle with that ourselves!). However, as kids enter the teen years, we need to pass the responsibility on to them (learning right alongside them if we haven't fully grasped the lesson ourselves!).

An important lesson in self-management is that everything has a "home." As the kids entered junior high and high school, I taught them how to set up a file system in their room. Their first file box or drawer had files for pictures, school papers to save, youth group information, 4-H fair information, and magazine articles. As they've grown older they've added files for work, college information, school clubs, and mission trips.

Adults have to keep insurance records, bills, financial statements, and taxes organized. Teenagers need to see how to keep personal papers and information available at a moment's notice. This will be a skill that will serve them their entire life.

In the Farrel home, when the boys started T-ball, I made a rule: Mom is not your equipment manager. I created a bin for each son, and all sports equipment was to be kept in the bin. As they got older (fifth or sixth grade) I began to entrust their important school and youth group papers to their care. In junior high, as a rite of passage, they receive their own personal organizer (such as a Day Runner or a FranklinCovey planner). And by the time they leave for college, I teach them how to use Microsoft Outlook to keep track of dates and activities and to schedule time on their calendars to *do* the work and prepare for the events.

Some kids love this rite of passage: their own calendar! I received my first one in sixth grade, and I've been addicted to planning and goal setting ever since! My niece made sure all the relatives knew that she wanted a "real" organizer system for her present her senior year. Organization may begin with the planner the school provides in September, but a smart parent will build on this with files, in- and out-boxes, desk sets, and personal organization systems. Her teens will head out the door to college or career ahead of their peers in goal setting and organization, giving them an edge in the job market because they will be able to get more done in less time.

Cooking

Several years ago, in the Savage home, we experimented with putting each of our teenagers in charge of a meal on a weekly basis. This was a meal they planned, shopped for, fully prepared, and cleaned up after once a week. The experience had multiple benefits. They learned not only to shop wisely but also to prepare the food. They also learned how time-consuming meal preparation is and how valuable some help can be. And they found out that dinner doesn't really end when everyone is done eating. The cleanup must be done before the kitchen is really closed!

Another family I know has designated one child a day whose job is to set the table and help mom prepare meals. This helps the children become comfortable in the kitchen and reminds them that everyone who eats has to help with meal preparation. In the Farrel home, all the sons had to learn in junior high how to cook for themselves and the family. Often, one son would stay home to make dinner while the rest of us went to a game, and we all rotated so Mom and Dad could be fans for all the sons as much as possible.

Several years ago, the Savages made a switch in our family meal responsibilities. We originally had one child designated as Mom's assistant for meal prep and cleanup, but we decided to have everyone help with cleanup until the job is finished. This includes clearing the table, wiping the table, loading the dishwasher, washing any dishes that need to be washed by hand, wiping the kitchen counters, and sweeping the floor if necessary. When we all work together, the job gets done much faster, and everyone can move on with their evening. I've also found that these new habits carry beyond our family. When visiting grandparents or being a guest in someone else's home, helping clean up after dinner is good manners.

The Handyman (or Woman)

Being a little self-sufficient is a great asset. Teach tweens and teens how to change light bulbs, hammer nails, and use a saw, screwdriver, and drill. I (Pam) am glad my mom taught me "righty tighty, lefty loosey" so when I use a screwdriver I have a clue what I am doing! My mother taught me how to refinish furniture, set a table, rake the lawn, plant (and weed) a garden, care for animals, mow the lawn, fix broken tools and appliances, and create something for someone out of next to nothing. Life is more than books and tests. As important as academia is, if you are a PhD and your car gets a flat where AAA can't help you, you are stuck unless you can change the tire! If your husband isn't handy or if you are a single mom, sign up your tween or teen for a 4-H club, a school shop class, or a summer enrichment course.

Driving

Teens may resist taking on some responsibilities, but every teen looks forward to one rite of passage. But this responsibility is a life-and-death issue: driving! In the Farrel home, before our teen can drive, he has to complete not only the state requirements but ours as well. He must know how to change a tire, check the oil, and handle the social obligations of driving. He must also complete a driving contract. We simply type questions into a file on the computer and then ask him to answer them, bring the answers to us, and discuss them. These are some of the questions:

- Who will be in the car with you?
- What rules will you give your friends to ensure everyone's safety?
- What if someone isn't obeying the rules?
- Who pays for gas? For insurance? For upkeep? For tickets?
- What will you do if you aren't driving and a friend is drinking?
- What will be your sources of distractions from driving safely, and how will you address them?
- Who will pay for your first car?
- If you share a car with a family member, how will you work out who drives it when?

Then we ask them to write out their own consequences if they break their own rules. Having all the details written down ahead of time keeps the arguments and conflict to a minimum.

At the Savage household, on our kids' sixteenth birthday, we give them the "Ten Commandments of Driving." It's a humorous yet instructional way to talk with your kids about guidelines for the privilege of driving.

1. Thou shalt pick up your trash in the car every day.

2. Thou shalt pay for your own gas (outside of school transportation).

3. Thou shalt check the oil regularly.

4. Thou shalt pay for half of your car insurance.

5. Thou shalt follow all laws.

6. Thou shalt wear your seat belt and require that all passengers do the same.

7. Thou shalt keep your eyes on the road. Never try to change a CD or a tape, answer a cell phone, or pick something up off the car floor while driving.

8. Thou shalt give the car a bath regularly.

9. Thou shalt still ask permission to leave the house.

10. Thou shalt remember that driving is a privilege that can be revoked at any time.

K.I.S.S.: Keep It Simple, Sweetie!

Often you can boil down proper behavior and decision making to a few key principles:

1. *Treat others how you want to be treated.* Put yourself in the other person's shoes. Luke 6:31 says, "Do to others as you would have them do to you."

2. *Don't be selfish!* Philippians 2:3-5 explains, "Do nothing out of selfish ambition or vain conceit, but in humility consider others better than yourselves. Each of you should look not only to your own interests, but also to the interests of others. Your attitude should be the same as that of Christ Jesus."

3. *Be nice:* Colossians 3:12 makes it clear: "Therefore, as God's chosen people, holy and dearly loved, clothe yourselves with compassion, kindness, humility, gentleness and patience."

 ### *From the Heart*

I recently gave my mother a gift I know she will treasure. I wrote her a tribute that I framed and gave her for Christmas. The words I wrote gave honor to her as my mentor. Here is an excerpt:

> Mom, you have been a foundational source of encouragement, faith, and hope in my life. From my earliest recollections, you were present and selfless in helping me achieve my dreams. You have modeled godliness and integrity in all areas of your life...
>
> I remember the way you fostered a friendship with "Grandma" Rosa and Rosina, who lived across the hallway in our apartment building, planting in me a love for those whose culture, lifestyle, and language might be different from mine.
>
> Our home was always open to whoever needed a meal or a bed. Guests were friends whether you knew

them or not. You truly operated by the saying "My home is your home."

You showed me how to make my marriage a priority by not hesitating to get a sitter for us so you could accompany Dad on a business trip or attend a special event together.

Now I am a mother, and through my almost 20 years of mothering I have found myself doing many of the things I watched you do. You may have never intentionally instructed me how to be hospitable, but you modeled it in your everyday actions. You rarely spoke about extending grace to others, but you did so every time one of us made a mistake and you had to clean up the mess. You have lived and mothered without giving out shame and guilt, something many women never accomplish…

Thank you for being the woman that you are. Thank you for being a woman after God's own heart. Thank you showing me how to be a wife and a mother. For that and more, I am eternally grateful.

I love you, Mom.

I also wrote a tribute to my dad the same Christmas. It was a very powerful and emotional exercise for me. It was a very emotional gift for them to receive as well. As I wrote these tributes, I was struck by the impact of what they did—even more than what they said.

We've talked about all kinds of strategies for mentoring our teens, but the one strategy that will make the most impact on our children will be the life we model for them. A life of integrity, honesty, and grace will impact not only our children's lives, but the lives of generations to come.

The Next Step

Make a list of all the practical skills you think a son or daughter should have before he or she leaves home. Which areas do you need to work on? How can you help your tween, teen, or young adult gain these skills? When will you work on passing on this information? Will you be the teacher, or will you delegate some of the items?

A Mom's Prayer

God, please help me see what skills and traits I need to teach my teens so they can responsibly run their own home someday. Help me show them how to manage relationships in a loving way, using Your love for me as a guideline. Amen.

Becoming a Relationship Specialist

Sex, Dating, and the Guy-Girl Thing

We needed some coffee. The long night was about to get longer. At 3:00 AM we finally had all the teens who had been at our home for an after-homecoming dessert back to their own homes. We hadn't planned on being a taxi service for teens. But one of the teens had caused quite a change of plans.

Our oldest, Brock, sat still dressed in his tux, head in his hands, brushing away tears. I was on one side of him with my arm over his shoulder, his dad on the other side, a strong shoulder to lean on. Brock reeled off the list of dramas we had walked him through that evening:

"I did it right. I go on a group date, but my girlfriend leaves me at the dance and doesn't even bother to tell me. I have to call her parents and tell them, 'Your daughter ditched me, and I don't know where she is.' Then she finally calls, I drive her home and break up with her, and as she's crying, I'm feeling sorry for *her!* This is not the homecoming I had planned!"

The trauma! The drama! What parent hasn't consoled a teen who didn't get asked to dance at the eighth-grade party or wasn't invited to the prom? Who gives Mom wisdom when her daughter wants to date or even marry a person with no belief in God—or no visible means of support? How does a mom pick up a junior high boy's emotions if his manliness is made fun of, or worse, if the girls totally ignore him? Trying to pry open a boys' emotions sometimes takes a crowbar! And calming the emotional storm of a heartbroken teen daughter is like calming a hurricane.

Mixed Messages

There are so many messages: *I Kissed Dating Goodbye, I Gave Dating a Chance, When God Writes Your Love Story, Dateable*…On one end of the pendulum was one dad we know who interviewed all the college young men his daughter dated—and she was away at school!

On the other end are parents who are too permissive. According to T. Suzanne Eller in *Real Issues, Real Teens*, one in four teens will acquire an STD. Almost 30 percent of teen girls have chlamydia, and a teen has a 50 percent chance of contracting gonorrhea. Fifty-five percent of teens admitted to having oral sex.[1] This is the era of tweens and teens having an ex-President who engaged in oral sex with someone almost the same age as his daughter. They watch reality shows where people choose their mates on game shows, and they gather debased relationship advice from *Sex in the City, Desperate Housewives,* or *Queer Eye for the Straight Guy.* On the Internet they can be defiled daily with a steady stream of porn. *What's a mother to do?*

The Good News

Fortunately, fear doesn't have to rule our hearts because there is some good news! Because of abstinence education by schools, parents, and youth groups, the rate of teens having sex before marriage, abortion, and teen birth rates are all going down.[2] Researcher George Barna discovered that 82 percent of this generation of teens have a desire to have one marriage partner for life.[3] The Mosaic generation (those born after Generation X to the Boomers) views sex, dating, marriage, and family more conservatively—despite what the television shows are saying. In their hearts, teens still want one true love for life. And it's our jobs as moms to help them achieve this lofty goal.

A Relationship Contract

Caleb, the Farrels' eighth grader, had transformed over the summer from a boy who couldn't care less about girls to a young man who showered multiple times a day and walked around the house without his T-shirt on, looking to see if he could catch a glimpse of his budding muscles in the reflection of the windows. One day, he asked, "Hey Mom, when do I get to write my relationship contract?"

When Bill and I were serving in youth ministry before we had children, we noticed that most of the arguments parents and teens had centered around only a few issues: money, lack of responsibility, and relationships. We started having every student write a relationship contract as a part of the yearly relationship conference we taught for teens. When given the opportunity to create their own rules and regulations for relationships, teens actually had fewer arguments with their parents and made wiser choices.

A Foundation of Love

Before you have your teens write a relationship contract, remember that they will be better off emotionally and will make better decisions for their life if they have a clear understanding that God loves them and wants what's best for them. It was not a bunch of rules that led Bill and me to make the wise decisions that rescued me from repeating negative family patterns—it was our relationship with God. The more I learned how much God loved me, the more I could trust the principles He laid out in the Bible, knowing they were for my good. As I realized God loved me so much that He died for me, I was motivated to step out and run relationships God's way. To warm up your teens, you might want to leave key verses about God's love for them on their pillow, mirror, or dashboard.

Don't spring the idea of a relationship contract on your teens if you are experiencing a tough time in your relationship with them. Try to introduce it when everybody's emotions are at a calm, peaceful level—or at least not during a screaming match! Prepare their heart with some great relational times first. Nothing beats quality fun family time—that is the best preparation for great tween or teen interaction with parents. Find some way to lighten up and laugh with them first.

When you talk about the relationship contract, tell them you'd like them to take responsibility for their own love life, so you have some questions you'd like them to answer. We recommend inputting the question into a computer file so your teens can respond right there. Then you can print them, talk about them, and edit them if you need to. Year after year, at the same time of year, you can ask your teens to pull the file up and add any new questions or concerns.

We call it a relationship contract because it isn't just about dating but about treating the opposite sex appropriately and learning to select a life partner. Like a rudder or compass, it should help guide them through the relational waters of young adult life and land them safely on the shores of a marriage with a healthy life partner. You can download a sample relationship contract at www.masterfulliving.com.

Now What?

What kind of results can you expect? Anything from a child copping an attitude ("This is dumb!") to a child who writes a term paper on relationships!

Six weeks after one of our sons wrote his contract, a girl started liking him. He immediately added two pages to his contract because he suddenly had more questions to ask and answer! For a different son, we added questions about how he was going to spot high-maintenance girls. He wrote, "I'll just know." Not an adequate answer—we sent him back to the computer. We let the guys know they didn't have to do the contract, but until they did it, they would get no use of our cars and no extra money from us for any social events. We have them revise their contract each fall—and no school shopping until they do. They always got it done.

To Date or Not to Date?

At the Savage household, we gave our teens the option of not dating at all. In grade school we used the term *game* to define boy-girl relationships at that stage of their lives. We told them that other kids in their grade would play the "boyfriend-girlfriend game" but that they wouldn't play it at such a young age. As they entered junior high and high school, we began to talk about the possibility of dating, but we included the option of not playing the game at all until they were old enough to be looking for a life partner.

Our daughter Anne decided to try the dating game with the boundaries we discussed and set together (similar to the Farrel's relationship contract). After two relationships, she decided she didn't need the distraction of dating and chose not to date through the remainder of high school. Our son Evan decided not to play the game at all. After attending a youth convention where he was challenged to "crush the crush" and consider not playing with the emotions of the opposite sex, Evan made a commitment not to date until he turned 18. He's appreciated how that decision has simplified his life during his high school years.

When Anne began to date, we took her out for a special dinner and gave her a purity ring to be a visual reminder of her commitment to keep herself sexually pure until the day she is married and can enjoy the gift of sex in marriage.

Parents need to avoid thinking that they need to have "the talk" with their preteens and teens. Rather than having one talk, we need to be talking with them openly about relationships, sex, purity, good choices, and their changing body all the time. If their friends are talking about those things 95 percent of the time (and they are!) and we are talking to them about those things 2 percent of the time, who will have the bigger influence? We should be their source of information and education, and they should feel very comfortable talking with us.

Modesty

Several years ago my (Jill's) oldest daughter was asked out to her first high school homecoming dance. She was excited at the prospect of dressing up, going to dinner, and being with friends at the dance itself. Of course, one of the first things we did was shop for a dress.

Financially, the hunt for the right dress was a challenge. We eventually found one on a JCPenney clearance rack that was just perfect. However, defining "just perfect" took some doing.

What was the issue at hand? Modesty.

Modesty isn't discussed much in today's society. Webster's dictionary defines *modest* as "observing the proprieties of dress and behavior: decent." Bluntly, it has to do with the amount of skin showing.

Today's "shrink-wrapped" fashions make modesty a challenge. Young women want to be in style, look their best, and wear the latest fashions—but what about young women (and their parents!) who believe that modesty should be taken into consideration? When shopping for a homecoming dress, my daughter kept pulling out dresses that were indeed very beautiful—at least what little dress there was to consider. As we continued to shop I began to realize that I had information that my daughter did not have. I knew that men and women are drawn to what they see (skin!) and what that visual stimulus does to their mind and their body. Don't get me wrong— that's a really good thing in a marriage relationship. God knew what He was doing when He created us as sexual beings! But a young woman must learn to keep unique aspects of her femininity for one man— her future husband.

Why does Victoria's Secret have large pictures of half-naked women in the windows of their store? Why does Abercrombie and Fitch use large sensual pictures of men and women showing large amounts of skin? They do that because it brings about a response in consumers. Sometimes it's a physical response, sometimes an emotional response, and they are hoping it will be a financial response as well.

So how do parents help their daughters (and sons!) choose modest clothing? Here are some ways to approach the subject.

- Avoid "do as I say, not as I do." In other words, Mom needs to evaluate whether what she is wearing is modest.

- Have a frank discussion with your preteen or teenage daughter, explaining to her the power of modesty and the effect of immodesty. Revisit that discussion often, explaining the implications of immodesty rather than just giving rules.

- Define limits. What about cleavage, bare bellies, short shorts, spaghetti straps, and bare backs?

- Make a game out of finding fashionable yet modest clothing. Go through a catalog together, making note of the cute clothing that fits a modest mind-set.

- Go window-shopping just to see how many outfits you can find that meet your family's standards. Select two or three outfits that your daughter can add to her closet.

Being modest in today's fashion culture may be a challenge, but it's not impossible. We parents can lead and equip our children to make good choices in the clothing they wear.

Getting Dad Involved

If you are married, or if you are single but your child's father is in the picture, there are several ways to get Dad involved in your child's relational life. My friend Doreen Hannah has a Bible study curriculum called Celebrate! You're the Daughter of the King,[4] which outlines a series of meetings where girls study their value from heaven's perspective. At the end of the series, Dad comes to a special event where he blesses his daughter and places a tiara on her head. Another version of this is the Dad's and Dolls Dance (or Dinner) which is a prom or dress-up dinner the fathers give for their daughters to teach them how other gentlemen should treat them.

Boys are not quite as into dress-up affairs. Instead, Bill takes the Farrel boys on a father-son trip every summer, so he has a perfect built-in "guy time" each year. When the boys were in second or third grade, Bill explained proper ways to act, talked about body parts, and distinguished bad touch from good touch. Then in a talk that happened sometime between fifth and seventh grade, Bill talked to the boys about wet dreams, masturbation, and how to handle thoughts of lust. About that time, I gave a basic hygiene pep talk as I gave them their own new travel kit with soap, deodorant, shaving supplies, shampoo, conditioner, and aftershave. Bill had a conversation with them about abstinence and why it is better than other methods of birth control, and I talked to them about the proper way to treat women (including "no means no!"). Bill also covers this as well because a man's reputation can be tarnished by accusations even if they aren't true. (Our sons do not babysit boys or girls alone.) Bill talks to the boys about rape laws, sex with a minor, sexual harassment, lewd comments, and how to be like Joseph and flee—leaving your coat behind if you have to!

Before high school, Bill does a "girls are awesome" talk. He distinguishes between high-maintenance and low-maintenance women. (We tell the boys, "The less clothing a girl is wearing, the more emotional baggage she might be carrying!") When Brock was 14, Bill wrapped his arms and a leg around Brock, got right in his ear, and said, "Brock, most women are awesome, a few are like leeches. They wrap themselves around a man and suck the life out of him. And this is how you spot those high-maintenance women…" It was very effective, so all the boys now get the "Klingon" talk. From this point on, either Bill or I could talk with the boys about almost any topic.

One family we know of had Dad handle instruction about sexual temptation, lust, and the draw of pornography by meeting once a week with his teenage son after school to study the book *Every Young Man's Battle*.[5] This gave father and son a resource that stimulated conversation about challenging topics. The son had been visiting websites he should not have been visiting. (The parents were using a software called Cybersitter to monitor where their children surfed on the Internet.) After discovering where their teenager had been and discovering that he had learned the password to remove the protective filter on the software, they became more diligent about addressing the issue and changing the password regularly. Both father and son benefited from this regular, honest time spent together during their son's sexually formative years.

Something's Not Right

Usually when I am concerned about something in our kids' relational life or have a gut feeling that something is wrong, I am right on the money. We parents should ask the hard questions so often that hearing them becomes normal. Everyone, parents and teens, need people to hold them accountable. Modeling accountability in our own lives buys us permission to hold our kids accountable in their lives as well. Bill asks the boys, "How's your thought life?" or "If I checked your computer history, would I like to see where you've surfed?" I ask, "Are you treating your date in a way that will make her mom and dad appreciate you?" Other times I asked a lighthearted question: "So did you do something today to make your mamma proud?" But my usual question is this: "How can I pray for you and (the girl) today? Got anything on your heart I can pray about?" I can gauge their integrity right away by their response (or lack of one). The key is asking in a way *that is not based on fear.* Don't assume the worst, or you'll sound like the police. Ask with confidence: "I am sure you and Hannah are making great choices because that is just the kind of guy you are, but I was wondering, is there anything I can pray for?" If they say no, then I usually say something like, "Well, you two have been dating for several months. How are you doing with your relationship contract commitments?" or "When Dad and I had been dating that long, we started to ask questions like... Are those things that have crossed your mind?"

Add Some Fun!

On a Farrel boy's sixteenth birthday, we take him to lunch (his choice of place, of course). That day we give him a few gifts: a key chain and a key to the car he will be driving, an ID bracelet, and an envelope. In the envelope is a blank driving contract (see chapter 3). The key chain and bracelet are inscribed on one side with Until the Day and on the other side with 1 Thessalonians 4:3. This verse says, "It is God's will that you should be sanctified: that you should avoid sexual immorality." Until the Day means he will wait for sex until the day he marries. Many parents give purity rings, and today, as a direct result of the growing number of quality abstinence groups, many nice rings are available at your local Christian bookstore or on the Internet.

We approach all behavior topics with a can-do attitude. This lunch isn't the time to scare our son straight; it's a celebration of good decisions so far and great decisions to come.

Addenda

Each year, the relationship contract might need revision to address new questions about relationships and new family traditions. Who pays for what on dates? When can a girl come on a family activity? (We almost always allowed the boys to bring female friends because we like to get to know them!) At what age do you go from group dates to double-dating to single dating—and what if none of the friends have girlfriends, so there's no group? At what point do you call someone a girlfriend? And what are the responsibilities of that relationship?

Then more serious talks arise: How do you break up in a way that allows you to still be friends with the young lady and her family? How do you know if this is "the one"? And we still have some biggies ahead: How do you propose, how do you stay pure while engaged, and how do you choose a pre-engagement and premarital counselor? The key to success in this area with your tweens, teens, and college students is to stay one step ahead of them!

You know you have hit a home run when your older teens are making wise choices, yet they still ask for advice from you and others who are leaders in the field. We've had a lot of late-night talks (why do they always want to talk about deep life issues in the wee hours of the morning?), but those late nights have paid off. We have full confidence in our oldest son's choices. We have a few late nights left with sons two and three because they are younger and still in process...so please pass the sugar, I need it for my coffee. It might be another long night!

 ### *From the Heart*

How can you be a relationship specialist if you didn't make good choices when you were a teen? What do you say to your teens when you can't use your life as an example for the choices you are asking them to make? How much do you tell them about the mistakes you made? Both Mark and I have had to face this challenge with our teenagers.

By the time Mark and I met, we had lived promiscuous lives. We did not save ourselves for marriage. We made decisions for Christ after we had started dating each other, but by that time the damage of promiscuity had already been done.

We determined that as parents we would not keep our past from our children, but we wouldn't offer the information either. If they asked, we would be honest. Eventually they asked, and we responded with honesty.

We realized that we could set examples even through our poor choices. We focused on the consequences we experienced because of our relationship choices. We shared how we not only paid physical consequences (STDs and sexual baggage in our marriage relationship) but emotional consequences (such as trust issues and false desires) from which we hoped our children could be spared. And because our marriage was very challenging at first (and we'd been open with our kids about that), we emphasized that the difficult challenges we faced in our first ten years of marriage were direct results of the poor choices we made in previous relationships (and in our relationship) before marriage.

We have been able to share that God's guidelines for relationships are not meant to squelch our fun but to protect us from the very consequences with which Mark and I had lived. Our kids never said, "Well, you had sex before marriage, so I can too." We were able to be examples of what happens when we live outside of God's plan for healthy marriage relationships.

One of the wonderful things about God is that He is able to take our poor choices and redeem them if we'll let Him. In this case, God took our poor choices and redeemed them by allowing us to share with our children the realities of living outside of God's ways. Don't be afraid to be honest with your teens. They may be initially disappointed to know the mistakes you made, but your relationship will be stronger when they know they can trust you to be open, honest, and willing to let them learn from your mistakes.

The Next Step

Have your teens complete a relationship contract and discuss it at a special event created to honor them and their future relationships.

Take your teens out on a date where you share the story of how you met and fell in love. Share how you knew you were meant to be together. They need to hear your story. They need to remember that you were once a teen who had issues, fears, frustrations, disappointments, and heartbreak. Use your love and your experience as a springboard to launch them into their relationship world.

A Mom's Prayer
Lord, help me encourage my teens to have a pure heart
before You. Help them choose a life of integrity. Help them
treat others as they would want to be treated. Amen.

5

The CFO

Teaching Teens the Value of a Dollar

A young woman met a young man at Bible college and fell in love. The romance grew, and eventually the young man decided to ask the girl's father for permission to marry her. The dutiful father quizzed the young man on his ability to provide for his precious daughter.

"I understand you don't have a job yet. How will you provide for my daughter?"

"God will provide," the young man responded piously.

"What if the car breaks down?"

"God will provide."

"And when she needs new clothes?"

"God will provide."

"And when the bills come due?"

"God will provide."

Later, his wife asked, "So, how did it go?"

"He seems to be a nice enough young man—in fact, I've never been shown such respect."

"Really?"

"Really. He thinks I'm God!"

We want to raise kids who have a good sense of faith and fiscal responsibility. Financial disputes are the number one reason for divorce, so we need to spend more time training our kids to be responsible stewards. And some of us do, while others of us feel a bit intimidated by the entire topic. Ellie Kay, author of *A Woman's Guide to Family Finances,* says the best way to teach our tweens and teens how to manage money is to learn to be wise money managers ourselves. In her book *Money Doesn't Grow on Trees* she lists some core values all teens should have in place before they fly the nest. The extended quotes in this section are from her book.[1]

1. The Value of a Work Ethic

Having a good work ethic means working hard and finding pleasure in a job well done.

Teens often try hard, but sometimes even then they just don't get things exactly right. A teenager wanting to earn some money decided to hire himself out as a handyman and started canvasing a wealthy neighborhood. He went to the front door of the first house and asked the owner if he had any jobs for him to do.

"Well," the owner responded, "you can paint my porch. How much would you charge?"

The kid said, "How about fifty dollars?" The man agreed and told him that the paint and brushes he might need were in the garage. The man's wife, inside the house, heard the conversation and said to her husband, "Does that boy realize that the porch goes all the way around the house?"

The man replied, "He should. He was standing on it."

A short time later, the teen came to the door to collect his money.

"You're finished already?" asked the man.

"Yep," the teen answered, "and I had paint left over, so I gave it two coats. "

Impressed, the man reached in his pocket for the $50.

"And by the way," the teen added, "that's not a Porch. It's a Ferrari."

Tweens

Ellie offers this idea for helping your teens to develop a good work ethic.

This is the age where you can introduce the concept of "Do all your work cheerfully." The first time your child begins to grumble over having to fold a load of laundry (or other job) you can institute the following:

In our family, we are committed to helping you learn how to do a job well without grumbling or complaining. This will help you later in life. We are so committed to helping you learn this that if you complain when we give you work, you will automatically do twice the work until you learn to do it without complaining.

So when I ask Daniel to take out the trash and he grouses, "Why do I always have to do this? Why doesn't Philip help?" Then he takes out the trash *and vacuums the stairs.* Or when Joshua is asked to fold a load of laundry and stomps down the hall, throwing a hissy fit—he folds *two loads* of laundry.

All we have to say is, "Do I hear you complaining?" to get a response of, "Oh no, Mama! We're not complaining. I'll get to that laundry right away." This technique may not work for all children in all families—but it's worked on our five children at home.

Of course, getting tweens to work is easier if they have been raised to work. When my (Pam's) kids were preschoolers and in early elementary grades, training them to make their bed, sweep, vacuum, dust, and do the dishes did take longer than doing it myself, but I knew if I invested early, I'd get that time back when they entered middle school and high school. I was right. Like the Kays, we rewarded a good work ethic and a good attitude, and we set up consequences for grumbling, pouting, complaining, or procrastinating. We'd add time to the chore or double the chore or take away a privilege so our kids had time to complete the chore. We would usually say, "You can do this with a good attitude, and it will go quickly. Or you can do it with a bad attitude, and it will feel like forever. But either way, you will do it." If we assigned a chore to all three sons to work on as a team and we saw that one or two were working hard and the other was slacking, we'd reassign the hard workers to a different task or give them a reward or send them on an errand that was easier so the other son would have to carry his fair share.

Teens

> Once each of our teens hit that special number (13) they suddenly became an independent, emancipated person, full of self-knowledge and special rights. One of those inalienable rights was the "pursuit of happiness" [supposedly] coupled with "the freedom from chores"…
>
> Another factor that comes into play during these years is outside work for teens. It's important to make sure they have a safe environment and that you know and trust those people for whom your child works. It's also important that they learn to do their jobs well and with a good attitude.

When your child is old enough to work outside the home, sit down with him or her and make a job training plan. Every family system is different. Some families have all their kids get a job at 14 or 15 with regular weekly hours. Others see participation in sports or leadership in extracurricular activities as a way to learn a strong work ethic, so these families might look for other financial earning options like starting a business, working for the family business, or helping out with family responsibilities. We (the Farrels) identified the chores we would need to pay for if we had no children, and we decided to pay our children to do what we would have had to pay others for, such as gardening, car washes, some house cleaning chores, and childcare. But we required that they do the same level of excellence as we would get if we hired it out, or we wouldn't pay the same amount. A more excellent job meant better pay.

2. The Value of a Dollar

Knowing the value of a dollar means knowing how much work would be required to earn the money to purchase other goods or services.

Tweens

By the time your child is in this group, you can slowly begin to introduce the idea of how long it takes them, in allowance money, to earn enough to pay for an item they want. For example, they may say, "I want the Pirates of the Carribbean video game, it's really cool!" You need to respond, "How many week's allowance will that game cost you?" When they begin to look at items in light of the hours they have to work to pay for it, they begin to learn the value of a dollar.

Giving an allowance is one area of concern for many parents. Should you give allowances, or should your kids earn every cent they get? If you do give an allowance, what do the kids pay for, and what is included in your family budget? You might wonder how big most allowances are. In 1999 allowances averaged $3.74 a week for ages 8–9, $5.19 for ages 10–11, $9.45 for kids 12–14.[2]

Below is a recommended allowance scale from *Christian Parenting* magazine.[3]

Age	amount per week
6–8	$2–$5
9–12	$7–$9
13–15	$10–$14
16–18	$15–$20

Another way to set allowances is to give a weekly amount in dollars that equals the child's age in years.

You might be thinking, *Allowances! Pay for chores! We can barely make ends meet. It's food and rent and not much else. I can't even think about extras.* Don't let false guilt and shame keep you from believing you can still give your children a full and meaningful life. Todd and Lynn Zastrow, Hearts at Home financial experts, recommend you lavish kids with love, not things. They suggest five simple ways to express your love:

1. Make their favorite meal or dessert.
2. Seat them at the head of the table.
3. Mail them a card or letter.
4. Have an award ceremony for some achievement.
5. Give them a family keepsake with the story that makes it special.[4]

Teens

This is the age where they should naturally be equating recreational activities with hours worked. They could have one day at Six Flags that would cost them three weeks work at their part-time job. It's also a good age to begin to talk to them about some of your household expenses and obligations so that they can gain a greater appreciation of the value of a dollar.

As teens get older, you can discuss family financial decisions with them. For example, if your family receives bonuses, you could say something like this:

"We have a $1000 check. We also have some car repair to do and some dental work coming up. We often try to put some of our extra income into your college fund or our IRA. What do you think? I'd like your input." You would make the final decisions of course, but this kind of reality check helps a 16- or 17-year-old quit asking for $300 tennis shoes or a $500 prom dress! Even if money isn't as tight in your household, asking older teens how they might invest or spend a set amount of money will help them learn how to make wise choices later in life when their own money is on the line.

3. The Value of Budgeting

Kids need to learn how to develop, tweak, and stay on a budget in order to meet their financial objectives.

Tweens

Ellie Kay suggests creating "fun budgets."

> The fun budgets...can begin to include trips to restaurants. Estimate what it will cost to buy their dinner and add a bit of a pad to that amount. You will give your child the amount for dinner as their "budget" (they never spend their own money on a family outing). Be sure they know that they can keep what they don't spend. If they want to forgo dessert or drink water instead of soda, then they can pocket the difference.

This type of approach can also include fun budgets on trips to the zoo, a theme park, or for souvenirs on vacation. One final area that older middlers can budget is for school supplies. The parents will give their child the money and put them on a budget per semester. Let them manage the purchase of initial supplies as well as ongoing school necessities. It's amazing how your child will no longer "lose" paper and pens when its their "own" money that will pay for those additional expenses.

Teens

In the Kay household, teens manage these budgets as well as their own clothing budget.

> They will also be paying for most of their recreational expenses—outside of family outings. A teen should never have to pay their own way to a restaurant, amusement park or movie when he attends with his family. However, when he goes out with friends, he needs to be aware of the fact that this will come out of his budget.
>
> It's wise to have a regular budget meeting with your

teen once a month to help them tweak their budgets. You might need to remind them there is a prom coming up (recreation budget) or that winter is just around the corner and they'll need a heavy coat (clothing budget).

The Savages help each teen create a three-ring binder we call their budget notebook. This is where they keep track of allocated monies in their savings accounts for such things as clothing, insurance, and future events. We also help them create a paycheck worksheet to help them divide and budget each paycheck. You can find sample pages of a budget notebook at www.jillsavage.org.

4. The Value Of Saving and Not Spending

In addition to learning the importance of building up a savings account, kids need to learn how to find the best value on goods and services.

Tweens

Ellie has her tweens doing comparison shopping.

> If they want to save for a bike, CD player, video game, or other "big" item, take them to www.froogle.com in order to research the price on the item. Print out the best price and take it to the mall to compare with the department store prices. Each time they save money, encourage this by praising them for their efforts. Be sure to brag on them within hearing distance to other family members and friends.

In the Farrel home, we say clothes are better when they are on sale! Make it a game to see what "best buys" your tweens can discover. Give them your grocery list on the way to the store and have them estimate the total before coupons, or involve them in organizing the coupons for groceries, pizza, or other family expenditures. One mom rewarded her tween with the difference between the retail price and the savings, and that money went 50-50 to the child: 50 percent to college savings and 50 percent to spending money. The tween became an expert at using coupons!

Teens

The Kay kids are taught how to "conquer a store."

> Walk them through the sale racks and point out how a similar shirt or pair of shoes cost substantially more at full price. If they are on their own clothing budget, they are going to be more likely to learn how to get more for less money. You might even want to take them into your insurance agent's office and let him or her explain the difference in price for a youthful driver who has tickets and one who is a good driver. This teaches them that sometimes "saving" money is a result of good behavior and responsible living.

5. The Value Of Investing

Knowing the value of investing includes realizing that our financial future will not take care of itself. We must take care of it through the power of compounding interest.

Tweens

Ellie believes kids by this age need their own savings account.

> It's important to require that your child save at least 10 percent of their allowance each week. About once a

month, allow them to go to the bank with you to make their own deposits. You might even check with your local bank to see if they have a child friendly savings account such as a "Looney Tunes" account in order to make saving money fun.

If you cannot find a bank to start a savings account because the minimum is more than you currently have, then simply grab a coffee can, basket, or bottle and begin asking the family to toss in their small change once a day or each evening. It is amazing how quickly pennies, nickels, and dimes can add up.

Both the Savages' and the Farrels' extended families give savings bonds at Christmas and on birthdays. We encourage the tweens to write a thank you and let the parent, aunt, or uncle know how much they appreciate the investment in their future. We talk about what will happen when the bond matures: maybe they will buy a car, complete a graduate studies degree, or buy an engagement ring or a new home. Won't this extra money come in handy then? By helping them picture their own future, they can picture why investment is an important concept.

Teens

Ellie raises the bar for many parents of teens. "Depending upon the maturity of your teen, they should have a substantial savings account that would allow them to open their first mutual fund. There are junior funds that can be opened with as little as $200 to $300 and only require a monthly contribution of $25 to $50."

The teen years are a good time to learn the value of compound interest. Have teens research banks and savings institutions to find the one with the best rate of return. One family in our community buys their teens a share of their favorite company on birthdays. Hot companies can become hot investments: In-N-Out Burger, Krispy Kreme

Doughnuts, Nike, Under Armor, McDonalds, and Taco Bell would be some of our sons' favorite companies! High school is a great time to learn all the ways to invest, including real estate, stocks, bonds, savings accounts, IRAs, and money market accounts.

When I (Pam) was 14, I sold a lamb in a 4-H fair and deposited that few hundred dollars into a passbook savings account. Nearly six years later, when I was getting married, I remember thinking how glad I was that I invested that little bit of money instead of buying a stereo for a car or a few new clothes. That stereo and those clothes would have been long gone, but my marriage would last forever. It was an investment in an investment.

6. The Value of Delayed Gratification

Some of the best things in life are those you have to wait for.

Tweens

The Kay family plays the "three-day wait" game in order to teach their tweens the value of waiting before you buy.

> Tell them they can buy it in three days and mark it in your palm pilot that you need to come back to that store at that time. You'll be amazed at how many times the child has changed their mind and no longer want the item. Use this as a teachable moment to explain the idea of impulse buying and the value of delayed gratification.

The Farrels ask, "Do you need it?" meaning, "Is it something you have to have to succeed in school, life, or love?" The Savages talk about delayed gratification a lot. We went 17 years without any kind of cable television. Why? Because we couldn't afford it on our one-income budget. We explained to the kids that we had to delay what we wanted today for Mom to be able to be at home, which was an investment in their lives now and in the future. We also practice a "wait game," but we wait one week rather than three days. The principle is still the same: Wait a week before you make a decision to buy.

Teens

> [Delayed gratification is the value that] is going to prepare your teen for a life of financial freedom rather than bondage to debt. It is also going to come in handy when their peer group tempts them to sample drugs or take advantage of a promiscuous classmate. So often, financial skills are just plain character issues that manifest themselves in similar ways.
>
> If your child has a prepaid credit card in their pocket, they will also have the opportunity to learn delayed gratification and victory over the temptation of plastic. These cards are paid for by the teens' savings account and are limited by the amount they've paid into the card. They are kind of like a debit card for savings, but they look and feel just like a regular credit card.

7. The Value Of Sharing

Parents can show their kids how to hold material possessions, time, and financial resources with open hands rather than a closed fist.

Tweens

In the Farrel home, every year at Christmas, each child selects a needy child (someone we know or someone we heard about through Project Angel Tree) or a worthy cause and gives a "gift to Jesus." When the children were young, this money was part of the family's Christmas budget. When they were in their tweens, we asked them to contribute "piggy bank" money toward the project, and we matched whatever they had. As they entered their teen years and received money from working, we asked them to contribute as the Lord led, and we matched these funds as well. The Kay family adopts a Third World child as a family project and puts their own kids in charge of writing letters to this new friend around the world. The Savages have participated in Project Angel Tree each Christmas. We request the opportunity to actually deliver the gift directly to the family if possible. Each time our children have gone to the home of someone less fortunate, they have been reminded of all they have themselves.

Teens

Teens should actively minister to those in need through soup kitchens, mission trips, and fund-raisers for the poor, needy, and abused. Teens can be valuable leaders and servants for pro-life clinics, political campaigns, inner-city missions (when accompanied by adults for safety), hospitals, meals on wheels, nursing homes, local church ministries, and short-term missions.

8. The Value of Diligence

Diligent people follow through with a vision for excellence until a job is done.

Tweens

This is when you teach your children to finish what they started. "If they beg you to take ballet, then the agreement is that they will take it for a year—whether they change their mind mid-stream or not. If they are a pianist, then they need to make it to that first recital. A good family motto to adopt is: We will finish what we start." In the Farrel home, the boys had to wrap up each sporting season they started. Then they could decide on options for the next quarter.

Teens

Look for opportunities to encourage your teen to "stay the course" or "work the system" to garner the desired results.

In late elementary school, Evan enjoyed gymnastics. In junior high, he tried out for a spot on a competitive cheerleading squad and won a place on the team. The boys not only performed gymnastic stunts but also lifted the girls and served as the foundation for the pyramids they used in their competition routines. In only a few months, Evan began to see the drawbacks of the team: less than ideal team relationships, long practices, and most of all, hard work. However, we took this opportunity to teach the character trait of diligence and required him to remain a part of the team until the competitive season ended nearly a year later. We also talked about weighing out all aspects of an opportunity before committing to it. Many times throughout his teen years, we've referred back to lessons learned from his cheerleading endeavor and helped him carefully weigh all the components of a commitment.

9. The Value of Responsibility and Accountability

We are 100 percent responsible for our 50 percent of our partnership with others.

Tweens

In these years, your children learn that if they do not follow through on their schoolwork responsibilities, their grades will suffer.

You can help your child get organized, but there comes a point where you let reality be the best teacher—and you're there to capitalize on the outcome. For example, if your child has a major project due in their class and they procrastinate until the ninth hour—you aren't required to rush out and buy them the materials they need in order to complete the project.

Teens

There may be no more significant characteristic that you teach your teen than there are consequences for specific behaviors and attitudes. If your teen understands that there are certain responsibilities they have in life then they will also learn that each one of these responsibilities comes with certain privileges as well as requirements. This means that when they forget to fill their tank with gas, then they run out. It also means that if they speed, they might get a ticket. We don't pay for their gas and we don't fight their tickets. Instead, we allow reality to be the best teacher and we use these moments as opportunities to teach the values of responsibility and accountability.

10. The Value of Rest

Kids need to know how to regroup and recharge without guilt.

What are you modeling to your children? Workaholic tendencies of all work and no play? Do you observe a Sabbath, a day off, a reward for a job well done?

Tweens

Tweens respond well to light at the end of the tunnel. Offer to take them to 7-Eleven for a Slurpee after they rake all day, or to the mall after they clean their room. My (Pam's) mom could get all of us to muck cow and sheep stalls all day with just a promise: "We'll go to town for a rootbeer float!" A reward at the end of a long day's work is a welcome prize that will keep morale high in your home. It takes so little to motivate most tweens!

Teens

The average teen lives a thousand miles an hour! School, rehearsals, practices, work, volunteer work, term papers, phone calls, youth group—meetings, meetings, meetings! They need a break! They need a nap! They need a vacation! They need a day off too!

Let your teen sleep in on vacation (or an occasional Saturday morning!). Encourage him or her to unplug on occasion: turn off the cell phone, get away from the computer, turn off the TV, and leave the portable CD player at home. You may get a little flack for encouraging a little peace and quiet, but being at peace with yourself is a lost art. Just as you train your teens to work hard, save money, and succeed, also train them the art of enjoying a quiet moment in front of the fireplace, drinking in the magic of a good book, and experiencing the calming renewal of a quiet walk in the forest or along the beach. Teach them the value of "white space" or "margin"—time to think, pray, or rest.

Our (the Savages') very social teenagers have to be reminded to be home at least one or two evenings a week to maintain balance in their life. They will go, go, go and then crash if they don't have some downtime. Often we have to "help" them to honor that time, but we've begun to see them make some responsible decisions in making time for rest and relaxation in recent months.

Increasing Our Own Financial Finesse

In all these vital areas, our tweens and teens will learn more from our example than from any book or words of advice we might offer. To teach our kids about money, giving, and saving, we have to be willing to learn about finances and stewardship ourselves. My (Pam's) friends who are most comfortable with this area of life are women who have proactively sought out information. One resource that helps you learn to see your money from God's point of view is Crown Financial Ministries' Bible study series. This course is made for married couples or individuals and is taught in a small-group format so you have emotional support to make some life changes. (Check out www.crown.org for great financial resources.)

Obedience is the key to God's favor and blessing. Some people think they will get God's attention if they do something grand or sacrificial. But 1 Samuel 15:22 says, "Does the LORD delight in burnt offerings and sacrifices as much as in obeying the voice of the LORD? To obey is better than sacrifice, and to heed is better than the fat of rams." A daily, moment-by-moment life of obedience pleases God. So when we handle our finances in an obedient manner, God's good hand will be on that area of our life too.

When the older Farrel boys were tweens, I bought banks with compartments for savings, spending, investing, and tithing. We taught the boys that a dollar should be split these ways:

- Tithe : 10 cents
- Save: 10 cents
- Invest: 10 cents
- Spend: 70 cents

When Times Get Tough

Things don't always go perfectly. Layoffs, job changes, illnesses, business failures, and economic downturns are just a few things families have to deal with. At what point do you share your economic issues with your tweens and teens? We think it depends on what you share, how many details you share, and your attitude when you share it!

Here are some guidelines to consider when you need to share economic information:

Share enough to adjust expectations. When a friend of ours was laid off, he and his wife explained to their children that Christmas was going to be different this year. They asked the kids to brainstorm ways to make Christmas special and not spend any money. They decided to make gifts and to serve Christmas dinner at the homeless shelter. They made cookies and candies, they wrote poems on homemade cards, and they remembered they were the fortunate ones because they had a roof over their heads. Now that Dad is reemployed, that family still looks back with fondness at that Christmas.

Share with hope and expectancy. A positive attitude keeps fear and panic at bay. When you share with hope, you invite the kids into a miracle. When they see God step in and provide in supernatural ways, their faith is built.

Share with their age in mind. Sarah's husband was diagnosed with an illness that sidelined him for more than a year. They had insurance, but he had no income, so Sarah became the main provider. She adapted the amount of information she shared with each child. She asked the older two, one in college and one in high school, to get part-time jobs to cover as many of their own expenses as possible. Sarah was very honest with her college son, preparing him for the change in the family income and budget. He decided to come home and attend junior college for the year so he could also help out with home repairs and his siblings.

Sarah explained to her middle school son that Dad needed to rest, so she would need him to pitch in more at home and do a Sunday morning paper route with his junior brother before church.

Sarah increased her hours by a few each week and asked her ten-year-old to do a fun project to encourage Daddy. She delegated the coupon clipping and grocery planning to her youngest daughter. She read Ellie Kay's *Save, Shop and Share* with her daughter. The family began to save a few hundred dollars a month on food alone.

As Dad began to feel better, he worked on an at-home business, building his hours, his strength, and his self-esteem week after week. The family had a tough year, but it drew the family together instead of pulling them apart.

The Desk

Sometimes to build our faith, God steps in and does something amazing and unexpected. My friend Sarina is a single mother. Despite the court system's best efforts, Sarina sometimes didn't receive her child support checks. But God is a Father to the fatherless. Here is Sarina's story:

Each day after I pick my son up from school, we drive by a secondhand store. One day we decided to stop and make a quick pass through the shop.

At the back of the store was an interesting desk with a hutch of some sort. I must have circled it ten times before asking the manager about it. I offered $25 less than the price marked on it, but the answer was no. Apparently, a man had expressed an interest on Saturday, the day she put it out. She thought the man might come back and pay the full price. I was about to leave when the manager glanced out to the parking lot and said, "There's the man now!" Without hesitation I blurted out, "I'll take it!"

When I got the desk home, I noticed that the desk drawers were numbered and signed by a Piero Fornasetti.

A few weeks later I stepped into an art gallery and got to chatting with the owner. I asked her if she knew anything of Fornasetti. I briefly told her my story about the desk and asked if she had any idea about its worth. She said, "Oh, twenty-five to thirty-five."

"Do you mean hundreds or thousands?" I asked.

She cracked a grin, fluttered her eyes, and said, "Thousands, my dear. Thousands."

I contacted a few art dealers on the Internet, and one that responded just happened to be in Italy. The desk actually went back to the son of the artist! The money the dealer sent us was just the amount we needed for the year. I was in the middle of a career change, and God provided!

The greatest gift a mom can give her children is a calm faith, fully assured that God is who we have told them He is. Our attitude and actions speak much louder than our words.

 ## *From the Heart*

Two years ago we set out on a journey to add a child to our family through adoption. From a financial perspective, it made absolutely no sense. However, every one of us knew this was the direction God had for our family.

I said to a friend early in the process, "This is financial suicide." Her response was one that changed my perspective forever. She said, "Jill, our God owns the cattle on a thousand hills. He just needs to sell a few cows to make this happen!" What a perspective of truth! From that day forward, we began to watch God sell cows. And sell cows He did—through fundraisers, adoption grants, and the generosity of complete strangers.

One Sunday evening we were playing cards as a family. Six-year-old Austin was using a card holder that my grandfather had made years earlier. It was a simple block of wood with ridges cut in it to hold a hand of cards. Our oldest son teasingly said, "Hey guys, we could make these card holders and sell them to other families to make money to adopt Kolya." We all laughed at the idea, but then we began to realize the opportunity before us. We had asked God to show us how to find the money for the adoption, and this was the first of many answers to prayer. After a trip to the lumberyard and an initial purchase of two-by-fours, sandpaper, and paint, we began our project. Every member of the family worked late into the night for several weeks to make 250 card holders in time for the Hearts at Home conference in March. The older kids learned to use a saw and electric sander, and the younger ones learned to paint carefully. We sold all of the card holders at the conference. We were exhausted in the end but shared an incredible sense of accomplishment. Together we had raised $1000 toward our goal. God was selling cows!

Our oldest daughter was 17 at the time. One day she announced that she was going to do a fundraiser called "Cooking for Kolya." She put together an order form of our family's favorite freezer foods and sold entire meals as well as individual casseroles and pans of brownies. When orders came in, she both prepared and delivered the food. By the end of her three-month fundraiser she had raised more than $1500. One teacher paid $50 for a single pan of brownies that she was selling for $5 simply because he believed in her cause. God was selling more cows!

Over six months we watched God sell $34,000 worth of cows. It was an amazing journey of faith for our family. However, I think the best part of that season was working together to complete a goal and seeing the results of hard work.

Our children need opportunities to be a part of something bigger than themselves. Raising money for a world catastrophe, participating in Project Angel Tree at Christmas, sponsoring a child through Compassion International—all of these are ways to expand our children's world beyond themselves and to be an intentional CFO mom.

The Next Step

Consider the ten values we looked at in the first half of this chapter. Choose a few areas and make a specific plan for teaching your teens those values.

A Mom's Prayer

Lord, please make me a wise steward of Your money. Help me to be an example and to teach and equip my children to work hard, save, invest, and be generous toward those in need. Amen.

The Referee

The Art of Disciplining a Teen

One Saturday afternoon, our preteen son was to be one place when we found out he was somewhere else. Mark and I had a houseful of people when I received a phone call tipping us off that our son wasn't where he was supposed to be. (Thank goodness for parents who believe that it indeed takes a village to raise a child.) The one place in our house where Mark and I could privately discuss the phone call and our strategy was the guest bathroom. I said to my unsuspecting husband, "We have a parenting challenge." With a bit of a chuckle I motioned to the small bathroom and said, "Would you like to step into my office?"

Our discussion began with me briefing Mark about the phone call I had just received from a caring parent who was concerned about our son. Once we both had the same information, we determined that we honestly didn't know what to do with this situation, so we prayed and asked God for His guidance. Then we discussed our options, determined our strategy, and agreed on the consequences. Then we began to carry out our plan.

What Do You Do with Them?

When our children are young, we address their misbehavior with time-outs, removing a favorite toy, or occasionally spanking. But when kids are too big to turn over your knee, what's a mom to do?

In sports, referees enforce the rules of the game. As moms, part of our job is to set and then help others follow the rules. This part of motherhood doesn't give us a warm fuzzy feeling, but we'll feel great when we see our kids living disciplined, successful lives. Think of discipline as making disciples. When we punish, we dish out retribution, but when we discipline, we train our kids to make wise choices. This is why at the Farrel home we have this philosophy:

> I do, you watch.
> We do together.
> You do, I watch.

When our kids do something wrong and we realize we have not addressed this area, we do not punish them. Instead, we train them and set consequences for making bad choices after being fully informed. We like to set our kids up for success.

We should always remember the goal of discipline: to help our kids grow into respectful, loving adults. Teenagers are still learning lessons of respect, responsibility, and trustworthiness. They will make mistakes along the way. Sometimes they will experience natural consequences, and sometimes Mom and Dad need to issue consequences to help drive home a lesson.

Not every mistake teenagers make has to be punished, especially if they are sorry and repentant. We want their God-given conscience to provide natural conviction. When that happens, a conversation may be all that is needed to discuss lessons learned and a strategy for not making the same mistake in the future.

However, if conviction is not present in our teens, then imparting a form of correction that imposes consequences in some way may be necessary. This is where a mom needs to be very creative.

Creative Correction

Former actress and homeschooling mother Lisa Welchel wrote a book titled *Creative Correction* that is jam-packed with ideas for dealing with discipline. Lisa reminds us that what works for one child may not necessarily work for another and that we need to be creative. She says, "You love your children, and I love mine. So let's give each other room to try new things, learn from our failures, and find what works best for each of our kids."[1]

It seems that finding what's best for each of our kids can be a full-time job for a mom. Sometimes we hit the nail on the head the first time with an effective correction, and sometimes only through trial and error do we find what works for each situation or for each child.

When one of our (the Savages') teens refused to keep her bathroom clean, we took "caution" tape and completely blocked the entrance to the room. We explained that since she wasn't being a good steward of what she had, she would lose the privilege of using the bathroom closest to her bedroom. For weeks she was forced to use a bathroom on the main level of the house even though her bedroom was on the second story. Eventually she recognized the error of her ways, came and discussed it with us, apologized, and committed to a new understanding of stewardship.

Address the Heart Issues

We moms often get caught up in addressing behavior issues with our teens, but when we do we may just be looking at the symptom rather than the problem. The outward behavior is representative of what's going on in the heart.

A child who consistently doesn't take out the trash even though he's supposed to may be dealing with *selfishness*. A teen who doesn't go to class prepared may have *laziness* in his heart. A daughter who thinks she knows more than anyone else in the house may be dealing with *pride*. If we address the outward behavior but never address what is driving that behavior, we won't stop the pattern. But if we can get to the root of the issue, we'll begin to see a true change of heart and then behavior.

Teens are capable of thinking deeply. We can help them identify sin issues in their own life. This is an important part of the correction process with teens, especially if they have a personal relationship with Christ.

In the Farrel home, we ask our teens questions to try to lead them to the right conclusion themselves. Asking questions helps make teens a bit less defensive, and they learn to ask themselves these same questions before making choices.

- Does this decision show respect for God? Respect for others? Respect for self?
- Will this choice benefit my reputation?
- Will it build a record of trust?
- Will it have negative or positive long-term consequences?

- How will this decision or behavior impact my family? My friends? My future?

Our goal is to talk less and get the teens to talk more. When they verbalize their choices, they often see the right choice.

Full Apology

In our early years, we (the Savages) realized that we weren't resolving conflict in our marriage. We weren't understanding the importance of a full apology.

Most of the time, we would just say, "I'm sorry." But that's just half an apology. A full apology is "I'm sorry for _____. I know I made you feel_____. Will you please forgive me?" The closure comes when the other person is able to extend forgiveness by responding, "I forgive you."

After learning and applying this to our marriage, we realized we needed to apply it to our family as a whole. We explained to the kids that we had never operated with an understanding of a full apology. We shared what we learned and set standards for handling future conflict.

When teens are belligerent to a parent, they need to make it right. When teens say something mean to a sibling, they need to make it right. When kids have a disrespectful attitude, it can't just be dropped. They need to clean it up relationally.

Short and Sweet

I (Pam) tend to be reactionary and emotional, so I have found it a wise habit to pray first, talk to Bill, and *then* talk to my teen. When I take this route, the conversation almost always turns out better because I can season my words with grace. Recently, I called one of my teens on the phone and caught him off guard with a plan for the following day. He was upset and reacted by raising his voice, listing all the reasons he was frustrated, and then hanging up without saying goodbye. It hurt me. I was sad, I was mad, and I wanted to yank all his privileges! Instead I prayed that he would realize that he handled the situation inappropriately. Within five minutes, my cell phone rang. "Mom, I'm so sorry. What I did just now was so wrong. You're a great mom, and I never should have reacted that way. Please forgive me." He didn't need any further punishment; God already taught him the life lesson needed.

Most parents want to lecture, and most teens shut it out. Teens want to know they are heard. They welcome respectful conversations. They rebel against long, raised-voice lectures.

Most of us lecture because we begin to feel out of control. But the more emotionally controlled we can be, the more influence we are able to have with our teen.

Working Together

Sometimes teens need to sort through their behavior themselves, coming back to Mom and Dad with some thoughts about what happened. We've often sent our teens to the computer (or a journal) with these questions:

- What did I do?
- Why was it wrong?
- How should I address the situation?
- Do I need to consider any root issues?

By giving them a few days to answer those questions and withholding privileges until they do, you help the teen do much of the work and do some self-evaluation. This provides a great foundation for discussion.

Kids will work to divide Mom and Dad. The pressures of raising teens can highlight the differences between Mom's and Dad's approach to discipline. One parent is more lenient, the other more strict. Two different people will approach parenting with different perspectives at times. The most important thing, however, is to avoid disagreements in front of your children. Allow yourself to "step into the office"— even if it's a nearby bathroom—to discuss the challenge and come to an agreement. This often takes compromise on both Mom's and Dad's part, especially if they approach discipline differently. Once a strategy is set, present a unified front. This sets a firm direction for your teens and lets them know you are in unity, you are serious, and you are unchanging.

One of the most effective things you can do is to tell your teens you don't know what to do with their misbehavior. Let them experience a bit of fear while you take up to 24 hours to determine what measures to take. Use that time to pray, meet with your husband, and determine the best steps to take to help your children learn their lesson. This sometimes helps them remember who's really in charge and that their freedom is now in your hands.

We've told our kids that we pray that if they make a wrong choice, they will get caught. And we remind them that God answers prayers.

One of the Savage teens made a decision to skip some classes one day at school. We found out and issued consequences at home. I kept waiting for the school staff to issue their own consequences, but several days went by and nothing happened. That's when my husband and I felt God prompting us to ensure that our teen would be caught.

We called the assistant principal, informed him of what had happened, and asked him to issue the appropriate consequences. The assistant principal said this was the first call of its kind for him. Most parents call and defend their teens, blaming the school rather than allowing the teen to experience deserved punishment. We, on the other hand, were requesting that our teen's behavior be addressed.

Other Authority

As our children become older they begin to have other authority figures in their lives, such as teachers, coaches, school administrators, and youth group leaders. The older our kids get, the more we have to learn to support other authority in their life. Our parental tendency is to protect our offspring, often letting the "mother bear" instinct kick in. However, when we do that by undermining other authority figures in our kids' lives, we are setting them up for failure in relationships, future employment, and responsible citizenship. Far too many teens hear Mom or Dad bad-mouthing a coach or teacher, taking notes on how to shift blame and divert responsibility.

Even if you don't agree with an authority figure in your teen's life, teach your son or daughter the value of respecting authority. We will not always agree with our boss, but we need to respect his or her authority. We may not see eye to eye with a coach, but we need to respect his or her position of authority. Don't undermine the authority of other adults in your teens' lives. Instead, model for them a respect for role and position.

Create a Way Out

Sometimes our kids just feel "stuck" in life. They look to us to help them out of a jam. They want to hear some ideas on how to handle issues—and deal with the consequences of their own poor choices. Once, Zach knew the girl he liked was not God's best for him. He fought with us for a few weeks, trying to justify the relationship, but when we asked the hard questions, he saw himself that the relationship just wasn't right. He didn't want to hurt her, so we brainstormed ways he could express his heart to her and redefine the relationship.

I let him practice and role play. The conversation went so well that now, years later, they are still friends.

We as parents might need to rescue our teens from the sea of their own emotions. Most teens really don't want to be depressed, annoying, or negative, but they sometimes can't find their way out alone. In some cases, you might want to consult a professional to help you plot a path of success with your teen. Don't make the mistake of confusing rebellion with depression. In a teen, these two emotions can sometimes look incredibly similar. Teens who are dealing with depression need to know that to seek emotional health with a trained counselor is a sign of strength.

Natural Consequences

By far, the best way to discipline tweens and teens is to let them pay the price for their choice. If they break something, they pay for it. If they procrastinate on a school project, don't bail them out—let them take the D.

Once, when one Farrel son was in junior high, he violated one of the standards he had set for himself on the relationship contract. He had begun the relationship correctly—he assured his friend and her parents that they were just "friends," meaning the physical contact would be just like any of his guy friends.

However, he was soon holding her hand and putting his arm over her shoulder. We told him we had observed this choice of breaking his promise and asked him what he thought God wanted him to do to make it right. He was miserable for a day. His friends were over, jumping on the trampoline, and he just went upstairs. He was in tears as he decided he needed to apologize for breaking the girl's trust and her parent's trust because he hadn't kept his word. Even though it was a small thing to most people, we let him struggle because he was laying a foundation for his future. Today it was just holding hands, but the stakes would be much higher in the future. We wanted him to feel the stress and responsibility of keeping his promises and experiencing consequences if he didn't. The next day he apologized to the girl, and then we drove him to her house to apologize to the parents. They were very gracious, but it proved to be a wise decision to let him wrestle with the consequences. Today, he is a responsible young man with great relationships and a high level of responsibility because he is an honest, trustworthy person.

 From the Heart

Dr. Kevin Leman says, "Remember, your job is not to make your child happy." Sometimes I have to keep that at the forefront of my mind because all too often I have to be the tough guy. I have to stand firm. I have to withstand the anger and emotions of a teen who doesn't get the big picture.

When young children experience discipline, they cry it off and move on. When they become older, they have an opinion about everything. They rationalize and argue. They can go days and weeks with a chip on their shoulder. That's when we're tempted to give in. We want to make life easier for ourselves by changing the emotional environment. But we can't do that. We have to stay true to our parenting responsibility of raising morally sound, respectful, trustworthy adults.

At the same time, most teens yearn to be listened to. They long to know they are heard and understood. When our kids are teens, we need to listen more than we speak. Work to draw them out. Ask questions more often than you give answers.

Let your goal be to be an influencer in your kids' lives. Gently lead and guide them along the way, showing them God's love all along the journey.

The Next Step

What areas of weakness do you see in your tween or teen? Begin praying that God would give you the opportunity to nip it in the bud. Select one of the options below to help address the issue:

1. Brainstorm options with your teen by asking questions.

2. Find out what the Bible says about the issue and initiate conversation with your teen.

3. Create a way out—a plan of improvement with your teen.

4. Interview other parents to find out how they have handled some of the issues you are concerned about.

5. Get some professional help.

A Mom's Prayer

Lord, give me incredible wisdom—Your wisdom—in dealing with my teens so they learn to make wise choices. Amen.

A Loving Shepherd

Supporting a Teen in Difficult Times

The call came in the middle of a meeting. We'd only been gone from the football practice field about 15 minutes when my cell phone rang, "Pam, are you sitting down? Caleb has been injured, and we think he needs to be taken to the hospital right now. Do you want to come, or shall we send for an ambulance?"

I was out the door and in my car before I even gave an answer. Caleb was white, clammy, and moaning in pain as we rushed him to the children's hospital. Bill carried his 13-year-old son—still in football pads—into the emergency room. Caleb was bleeding internally and spent the next few hours in tests and then in the intensive care unit. Nine months later he was up and running at full speed, but my world changed that day. I learned a whole new set of skills—I had to.

When we have to care for a child in emotional, physical, or social pain, we can draw strength from 2 Corinthians 1:3-4: "Praise be to the God and Father of our Lord Jesus Christ, the Father of compassion and the God of all comfort, who comforts us in all our troubles, so that we can comfort those in any trouble with the comfort we ourselves have received from God." On these next few pages, may you find the comfort you need as a mom to comfort and encourage your children. You may not need the information right away, but at some time, you will be the agent of God's shepherding comfort. Your children will look to you to be God's funnel of encouragement, hope, and comfort on their dark days. May you find hope and help from those who have been there.

Every Day Matters

Terminal. That is a word no mother ever wants to hear. My (Pam's) roommate in college, Cindy, heard it twice. Her firstborn, Amanda, died at birth. Later, she gave birth to a beautiful daughter, Erika, who shortly after birth was diagnosed with a terminal condition. Erika looked like a beautiful little Cabbage Patch doll. As a toddler, her blond hair flowed down her back. Her smile was contagious; her sense of humor was dry and witty. But she was also dying of spinal muscular atrophy. Still, Cindy was able to to love lavishly.

> At first, I could not look at Erika without the thought going through my mind that she was dying. We were just numb with grief and sadness. As time went by, I knew that I wasn't going to be the mom Erika needed me to be if I kept focused on death. In reality, we're all terminal. None of us know when our last breath on the earth will be, and we can't waste time fretting about it. So I started focusing on what I had to be thankful for, even though some days that was the mere fact that she was breathing! That changed my perspective and gave me more energy to do what Erika needed me to do.

Where did Cindy get the ability to go forward or even function day to day? How did she find the ability to navigate such devastating news?

> I think back to when to we lost Amanda in 1985, and I remember worrying that God was punishing me for all the rotten things I'd done in my life. I know now that came from warped views of God that I'd picked up even as a child. But it was the beginning of God working in my heart and life to set some things straight and begin to peel off the layers surrounding my heart.
>
> The biggest issue that God took up with me was my identity in Christ. It was time to finally get it right. My life was dominated by fear. I feared people, circumstances, the future, and even the past. I was angry because I didn't know how to cope with it. I started my journey of studying who I am in Christ and how God views me and all that He has done to make me His. It changed my life. As I meditated on the truths of God's Word it transformed me. It empowered me to live like God intended me to live. It gave me peace knowing that God was completely taking care of me no matter what the outside circumstances. I read through the whole Bible and wrote down every verse that told me how God loved and cared for me and carried it around with me and read it.

Going to Bat, Going to the Mat

While Jill and I were writing this book, a young man named Shawn, one of my son's best friends, was in a car accident driving home from work. His mother, Vicky, rallied a support group right away, and we prayed. Day after day we waited together to see if Shawn would pull through. One of her friends sent daily e-mail prayer updates. Shawn survived against all odds and was released to a convalescent hospital.

Vicky went into action: She asked questions, she requested clean sheets, she stayed in Shawn's room, she pushed for more rehabilitation work—she went to bat for her son. He was shrinking to skin and bones, and she told the staff, "Either you figure out a way to get him on solid food or tomorrow I will start feeding him myself!" Amazingly, the staff discovered a way to help Shawn swallow and eat, and his strength began to grow. Vicky talked to him, and she brought in photo albums, music, games, books…any resource she thought might help him regain his ability to walk, talk, and learn. (On Christmas Eve, after we had been out of town for five weeks, our doorbell rang. It was Shawn in his letterman's jacket, holding a Christmas gift for us—but the best gift was seeing his big bright smile and watching him walk again!)

I admired Vicky's tenacious, positive attitude when she was exhausted and bone tired herself. Vicky went to bat for Shawn over and over, never settling for the status quo or the easy way out. She went to the mat for Shawn in prayer.

Joy for the Journey

I (Pam) knew something was different about Becky as soon as I met her. She was upbeat, joyful, and enthusiastic. Many of us moms are exhausted and sometimes even exasperated, but Becky is exuberant.

At a dinner with several other women who knew Becky, the conversation around the table quickly turned to a consensus that they all wished they were more like her. I soon discovered why. She had learned to be positive, to choose to be joyful through some very dark days. Listen as she shares her story, starting with the birth of her long-awaited baby, Rochelle:

> Rochelle was a miracle baby. She arrived after eight years of prayer, visits to doctors, surgeries, and trips to fertility

clinics. When Rochelle was 18 months old, a doctor told us, "Your daughter has a terminal muscle disease. I just don't know which one." We began a medical odyssey that included a neurologist, a metabolic specialist, EKGs, lab work, a muscle biopsy, and still more appointments with doctors.

My hurt, confusion, and depression gave way to anger. I vividly remember rocking my daughter to sleep one night, looking out the window and shouting to God that He had failed us. He could have healed our baby, but He didn't! I told Him I no longer trusted Him, and I would be taking care of Rochelle myself.

Shortly before Rochelle's sixth birthday I had a "God encounter" that would forever change my life and heart. In my mind, God took me for a walk through the Garden of Eden. He told me that He had created the Garden for us, but that sin came into the world, and that is why some children are now sick and broken. God had not left me. I was angry and hurt and had left God, but He was still there.

Shortly after my "God encounter," we finally found out what Rochelle's disease was called: congenital myasthenia. We were thankful and relieved to find out that it was not a *terminal* muscle disease. But Rochelle's journey from six years to sixteen years has included two visits from our home in Oregon to the Mayo Clinic in Rochester, Minnesota, exploratory surgery, experimental medication, homebound schooling with a tutor, frustration that her body can't keep up with her sharp intellect, loneliness, low self-esteem, and feeling like she doesn't fit here on earth.

Coping to Conquering

Becky took some specific steps to walk alongside Rochelle and help her become—as one of the women at that dinner table said—"a mature, godly young woman, the kind you want your sons to bring home to marry."

Connect to Outside Help

Becky linked Rochelle to people that she could lean on, talk to, and hang out with.

> We have a church that doesn't get tired of our journey and continues to wrap their arms of love and prayer around us. Some show their love by sending notes of encouragement, others call, and many continually ask how we are doing…They are her best cheerleaders. Our youth pastors love Rochelle like one of their own children. They have come alongside our little family of three, learning and understanding what myasthenia is and does. Rochelle also has found ways to help and be a part of the youth group and its activities even with her health limitations. We are able to send Rochelle on outings with them since they know what to watch out for with Rochelle and to be sure she rests if she is getting too tired.

Connect to Service

Rochelle has learned from her mom that it's hard to feel sorry for yourself when you are giving to others. Rochelle works in children's ministries in her church, where she is able to experience success and the sense of accomplishment. The children's pastors have embraced Rochelle and her challenges. "It has been a gift of life for Rochelle, and she is a very dedicated helper," Becky says. As with many children dealing with serious illness, Rochelle has an "old soul," one with wisdom and perseverance well beyond her years. This wisdom can become a resource for others who are dealing with life's dramas and traumas.

Connect to Other Overcomers

Becky looked for role models for her daughter: Helen Keller, Corrie ten Boom, Joni Eareckson Tada, and Fanny Crosby. The outcome of this step has been profound. Becky explains, "Rochelle's walk with the Lord is strong...Her body may be weak, but her spirit is strong."

Hope begets hope. A special friend of Rochelle's who herself struggles with chronic illness and recently was diagnosed with cancer gave Rochelle a basket of hope. It contained poems and gifts that were symbolic of Rochelle's need at the time. For example, one was a box of Band-Aids, reminding Rochelle that God cared about her hurts—especially the hurts of her heart. According to Becky, "Rochelle came downstairs, crying and holding the Band-Aids and card. We both put Band-Aids on, held each other, and cried."

Connect to Hope

Becky has nurtured the talent and skills that Rochelle has; instead of focusing on what Rochelle can't do she focuses on what she can do. Rochelle can't do everything, but sometimes our hidden talents come forward when other abilities are taken away.

> Writing and journaling help Rochelle process life. Artistic endeavors like drawing and painting offer Rochelle a healthy diversion and take little energy to enjoy...
>
> The best way I can encourage Rochelle has been to really listen. I have been learning how to listen to her and not try and offer her answers. Right now Rochelle

needs us to listen to her heart and be with her as she wrestles with the myasthenia…She has the same hopes and dreams of any teen, but how the dreams and myasthenia fit will be played out in the unknown future. Steve and I have no easy answers, we listen, pray and at times the tears flow…We have to be very careful to be sure that she knows that we love her and that she isn't a burden. We often leave her notes by her bed so they greet her when she opens her eyes in the morning.

Hope for Mom

Becky has made sure she takes care of herself so she can care for Rochelle.

My personal path to healing the hurts and disappointment has been a process. After my "God encounter," I began reading books by Catherine Marshall and Edith Schaeffer, who have also suffered difficulties and wrestled with God. C.S. Lewis says, "We read to know we are not alone." I have found that true in my life. The Scriptures have been such a comfort when I can find no other answers…

God also began to gently prompt me to begin a journey of gratitude, and I daily began to look for things to be thankful for. It took my eyes off of our difficulties. I love what Charlotte Bronte says: "I try to avoid looking forward or backward, and try to keep looking upward." Gratitude journaling helps me to keep my eyes focused upward, where my help comes from.

Becky offers a top-12 list for moms dealing with a catastrophic situation:

1. *Get a Bible* you understand. Your lifeline—your life preserver—is the Bible. You can't flourish without God and His Word!

2. *Get a support system* in place. Ask friends to walk with you. Some will be there for the sprint, and others will be long-distance runners. God can use them all.

3. *Get prayer partners* who storm the gates of heaven for you and your family.

4. *Get a good strong church* to embrace you and your family.

5. *Get good doctors* who will answer your questions, make referrals, and suggest resources.

6. *Get a good counselor* to help you with your questions and struggles. The counselor should work with the entire family.

7. *Get some good books* in which authors share their personal struggles, difficulties, and successes.

8. *Get connected to other networks.* Good resource books regarding special-needs children are available through organizations like Focus on the Family. Find a medical association that deals with your child's specific affliction.

9. *Get informed.* Learn all you can about the illness your child faces. But if you are fighting fear and discouragement, take a break. When you have enough information, *stop* researching. Beware of overload that may produce depression or discouragement.

10. *Get an advocate.* Don't go to the doctor's appointments alone. If you are married, see if your spouse can go with you. If not, take another family member or good friend. Ask your advocate to take notes for you so you can focus

on the doctor, your emotions, and the conversation rather than getting lost in the details of the information.

11. *Get sleep.* Take time for rest and proper nourishment. Exhaustion makes cowards out of all of us.

12. *Get to a grateful place.* Don't forget to be thankful and smell the flowers. When you begin to worry, remember what Corrie ten Boom said: "I realized that worrying is carrying tomorrow's burden with today's strength. It's carrying two days at once."

Overcome by Outlasting the Opposition

Some of our children have illnesses or disabilities that can be overcome or at least adjusted to in order to live a "normal," independent life—if only we could get in touch with the right information, expert, or therapy. We may need to persevere to find those resources. My friend Linda is an inspiring example.

Linda's son, Jason, was a sweet, happy, well-adjusted child. However, in kindergarten Jason had difficulty learning the alphabet and counting to ten. Six weeks into Jason's kindergarten year, the principal recommended Jason undergo a battery of academic testing. He was diagnosed with dyslexia, dysgraphia, audio-processing and sequencing difficulties, and attention difficulty. However, God blessed him with an

IQ of 138. So Linda prayed…

She found a language therapist who not only taught Jason during his elementary years but also prayed for him, nurtured him, and loved him. When Jason was 12 years old and in sixth grade, Linda and her husband sensed God calling them to a geographic move. To a mother with a special-needs child and a strong support system in place, this can be petrifying. But instead of giving into fear, she prayed…

In Dallas, Texas, Linda found a Christian pediatric counselor who specialized in children with learning disabilities. He saw that Jason was becoming depressed because he wasn't able to perform up to his potential in school. As he entered puberty, Jason exhibited a hostile dependency toward Linda and her husband. Though Linda took Jason to counseling weekly for a year, his depression became worse. He slept most of the day after school. He became withdrawn, which was opposite of his personality. He grew more angry at his parents and blamed God for not healing him of his disabilities. He began choosing the wrong friends and started using drugs to self-medicate his depression. He lost his self-esteem and his will to live. His life was spiraling down week by week. So Linda prayed…

She enrolled Jason in a school for drug abuse and mental health. She also took him to a drug and alcohol counselor for several months. But eventually, the counselor realized Jason needed more intensive support and recommended that Linda and her husband meet with an educational specialist, who recommended five potential schools for Jason. So Linda prayed…

She made appointments at three of the five schools and flew to interview each of the directors. She and her husband were faced with the heart-wrenching decision to send their son away to a school in Utah. Linda found a pastor who had chosen the same path for his daughter, and while visiting with him over the phone, she realized this was the best option for Jason. So she prayed…

Shortly after Jason began attending the new school, Linda and her husband sensed that Jason was becoming emotionally healthy again. After six months, the school in Utah recommended that Jason attend a school in Connecticut that specialized in students with learning differences. Linda and her husband agreed to send Jason to Connecticut for his ninth-grade year. For the first time, he began to take responsibility for his learning differences and began to learn and succeed in school. Jason made good grades that year and came home for the summer. He attended a church youth camp and recommitted his life to Jesus Christ. Linda counseled with the camp speaker about where Jason should finish high school. The speaker recommended that Jason attend the local public high school and be involved in his church's youth group so his spiritual life would continue to grow. The speaker prayed with Linda and Jason, and they knew he was to stay home and attend the local public high school. So she prayed…

Linda kept in close contact with the special education specialist at the high school, who became Jason's advocate. Linda called the SAT office and arranged for Jason to take the SAT orally and have special accommodations. Jason graduated from high school, and his SAT score enabled him to apply to several colleges. So Jason and Linda prayed…

Jason chose to attend the University of the Ozarks in Clarksville, Arkansas, which has a learning lab for students with learning differences. He is a senior and may graduate cum laude with a degree in business management. He is free from depression and has a personal relationship with Christ. He loves the Lord and desires to help other young people with difficult situations to trust God and to never give up.

God didn't rescue Linda and her family *from* the circumstance— He walked them *through* it to victory.

Hope on the Hard Days

Sometimes our kids' injuries can't been seen. They aren't visible on the outside, and they aren't learning disorders. Some kids suffer internal emotional or social pain that can be equally devastating to them and hard for us to watch. Sometimes we wonder how we can shepherd our kids when we feel so drained ourselves. Single moms can especially feel this way. My friend Dana shares a story about how God helped her deal with the most painful holiday in her son's life.[1]

My two sons and I found the days before Father's Day no cause for celebration. Their dad and I had divorced shortly after 3-year-old Nathan's birth. Living just a few miles from our home, Dad often made arrangements to come see the boys, but then he would fail to show up and leave them waiting on the front porch...

We decided to spend Father's Day at Disneyland with some friends. Because we would miss church on Sunday morning, we attended the night before. I put Nathan into the preschool class and CJ went to "big church" with me. During worship service, CJ started to cry again.

When the pastor asked all the fathers to stand, his tears gushed. We walked out into the foyer, where I held him. A pastor offered to pray with us in an empty office. Despite CJ's many sessions of counseling, he said, "How come Daddy doesn't want to see me? Why did he leave us?"

I cried with him, and then we talked. "I have an idea," I said. "Let's spend every Father's Day celebrating the dad you're going to be some day. You'll get presents and cards for maybe 15 years!"

We discussed some of the qualities he wanted to emulate for his children. CJ named the first two on his list: reading the Bible and teaching his children to pray. So as CJ's first Father's Day gift, I gave him a dad's devotional

Bible in black leather with his name printed in gold. The next morning when my alarm went off at 5:45 to get ready for Disneyland, I found my son awake and reading his Bible.

CJ hasn't had a meltdown in months. He still misses his dad, but he's found a new focus. He discovered more than just knowing God as a good Father. He's learning to apply godly qualities to his life as well. He had listed "guidance" as one of the things a good father should give. Now he's experienced fatherly guidance firsthand.

Home Safe

As moms, we often wonder, *Who will shepherd me as I shepherd my child? Who will hold me up?* Janet Eckles, a mom who parented three children after going blind herself, knows firsthand who leads her, holds her, and pulls her through no matter what. Recently she told me a story about her son Joe.

My youngest son, Joe, accepted Christ when he was 17 years old. My heart was filled with joy, knowing that he had received his salvation and his place for eternity was guaranteed. But Joe would test us at times. When he was 19, he surprised us by coming home with a cross tattooed on his left arm.

I thought about that cross—and what it meant—five weeks later when the unthinkable happened. The phone rang at 2:30 AM. A few moments later our middle son, Jeff, ran into our room to inform us that Joe was badly hurt. My husband, Jeff, and I frantically rushed out the door and drove to the hospital where Joe had been taken. When we rushed into the emergency room, we received the heart-wrenching news: Joe had been stabbed several times, and he had not survived. The shock and horror of the death of my youngest son was more than I could bear.

God's Word became my anchor. "Be still and know that I am God" echoed in my heart. I focused on His promise: "My grace is sufficient." The words of the psalmist became my own: "The LORD is my rock and my fortress and my deliverer; My God, my strength, in whom I will trust."

Sometimes when I go by Joe's empty and silent bedroom, my heart skips a beat and wants to cry out his name. I rely on Jesus to steady me with His unique love and tenderness. He reassures me of the place where Joe is now. My heart hears Joe's voice saying, "Mom, remember when you used to call my friend's home to make sure that I was there and I was safe? You don't need to call anyone anymore…you know exactly where I am. I'm home, Mom, I'm safe."

Home safe—that's where God will bring you and your children. Regardless of what you are facing, regardless of what your child is facing, know that God is your Father and will shepherd you through life's harshest trials. And even in the most unthinkable and unwanted of circumstances, including an untimely death of a tween or teen, God will meet you in that place of pain and carry you through and forward. He's done it for Vicky, for Cindy, for Janet, for Dana, and for Linda, and He'll do it for you.

I remember talking to my roommate Cindy shortly after Erika passed away and went to heaven. I asked Cindy how she was doing. How she was handling such a hard life passage? I will always remember her reply:

"Pam, I have two choices. I can run away from God in anger and hold on to my own rage, anger, despair, and disillusionment. That's a dark place. Or I can run to God with my pain and find comfort, supernatural peace, hope, and even someday, joy. To me the decision was obvious though not easy. I choose Jesus and trust He will carry my pain now just as He did on the cross."

 ## *From the Heart*

Eighteen months ago, Mark and I added our fifth child to our family. Nine-year-old Kolya came to us through international adoption. After two trips to Russia we brought home our new son who knew not one word of English. Thus began my journey of being the mother of a special-needs child.

I prayed for God's direction in making schooling decisions for Kolya. Should we have him attend the public school, which has an ESL (English as a Second Language) program, or our Christian school, which doesn't have an ESL program but does provide a foundation of faith in every aspect of a student's education? Do we hire a tutor? What do I need to be prepared to do to assist in his education? I had so many questions that I knew only God could answer.

We eventually made the decision to go with the Christian school, which proved to be the best choice for Kolya. During his first year, the school's resource teacher spent hours with him each day helping him learn English and catching him up on math skills. Within months Kolya was mainstreamed into a second-grade classroom (two grade levels lower than his age-appropriate grade level) with regular visits to the resource room when the class focused on science and history, which were impossible for Kolya to deal with in his first year in America.

At home I cleared my schedule completely to allow for hours of extra work after school each day. Overwhelmed with the challenges of helping Kolya catch up, I asked God for creativity and wisdom, and God provided. He gave me games to play with Kolya when we drove to and from school to increase his vocabulary. He showed me how to modify studying strategies for tests for a child with limited comprehension. He gave me the courage to recommend educational and classroom strategies that best met his special needs. And He gave me a new friend, Tonya, who had a special-education degree and could give me wisdom and understanding in dealing with learning challenges I had never had to face myself or with any of my other four children.

Now, 18 months later, Kolya is about to turn 11 and is in his second year in school in America. Kolya is completely mainstreamed into a regular classroom, but I now find myself in the role of advocate. Recently the class compiled a cookbook of their favorite recipes to go along with their reading lessons for the month. Kolya has specialized reading lessons in the resource room, so the book was compiled without his contribution to the project. When he brought home the completed book, his hurt and disappointment were evident. The class project everyone had been so excited about was missing the contribution of one of the class members. I had to be his advocate as I met with the teacher to explain that she needed to be inclusive in modifying projects or assignments to include Kolya even when he may be at a different stage of learning or utilizing special educational resources at the school. The young teacher immediately saw the error of her ways and apologized for not thinking that through when working on the project.

However, being an advocate wasn't the only part I had to play in this situation. Shepherding my tween's heart to understand that people will disappoint us or hurt us unintentionally was the task at hand. We talked about what it feels like to be left out and how we can remember that feeling and try not to do that to anyone else. And we had the opportunity to talk about forgiveness and grace. I explained to Kolya that choosing to forgive his teacher for her oversight was the only way the hurt would really go away. Kolya just accepted Jesus Christ as his Savior several months ago, so this was a great opportunity to further understand the concepts of grace and forgiveness that we both receive and give.

God is called the Good Shepherd because shepherding is a part of His character. When you find yourself needing to care for the physical or emotional needs of a hurting son or daughter, trust the Good Shepherd to lead you in the steps of shepherding his or her heart.

The Next Step

Select one of the ideas below to move forward with your teen through rough waters.

1. Becky offered 12 steps to successfully navigate a crisis. What is one thing from her list you can do this week to better cope with your own stressful situation or to help another mother who is going through a hard time?

2. Linda helped her son overcome through a pattern of praying with other moms. Who can you pray with this week? (Join a Moms In Touch group [www.momsintouch.org], a Bible study for moms, or invite a friend over to pray.)

3. Dana gave a creative gift to her son. Is there something encouraging you can do for one of your children this week?

4. Do you know another mom in pain whom you might be able to encourage?

A Mom's Prayer

Lord, please shepherd me so I can shepherd my teen. Comfort me so I can give comfort. Go before me and send me the resources and connections I need to help my child. Amen.

A Life Preserver

Walking with a Prodigal or a Teen in Emotional Pain

Whenever we (Jill or Pam) ask an audience of their most important prayer requests, the overwhelming majority will write down the painful story of a prodigal child. A mother of ten children was asked, "Is it difficult for you to give the exact same amount of time and attention to every child?" Her reply surprised us. "I don't even try. My heart will always break first for the one who needs me the most."

I (Pam) have observed a pattern. If I have seen it once, I have seen it a hundred times in more than 20 years of working with women. All too often Dad makes a decision that deeply wounds a child. This decision (usually a series of decisions) often involves abuse, abandonment, addiction, or adultery. Dad is absent from the family when the consequences or repercussions of his choices show up in the children's tween and teen years. Mom is left to deal with the prodigal's pain.

My father abused alcohol and had a frightening rage problem. My siblings and I had a variety of issues to deal with as a result, and my mom's brave and tenacious resolve pulled us through. She reached out for help and clung to her value system. She also held on to me during the two years that I made her life worse. During that time, I knew Mom provided a safe place for me. I knew she loved me.

We (Jill and Pam) have found that *most* kids who lose track do so because either they have a strong-willed, "have to learn the hard way" personality or they have a wounded heart—usually because of an adult who let them down.

Why Do Good Kids Make Bad Choices?

Tim Kimmel, in his insightful book *Why Christian Kids Rebel*, lists eight key reasons good kids make bad life choices.[1] (We highly recommend this book if you are dealing with a child making poor decisions.)

1. They might not know Christ personally.

2. Traumatic experiences may have left them angry at God.

3. They may be mad at their parents' real or perceived shortcomings.

4. They may be pushed too hard to succeed.

5. They may be confused or disillusioned. They may be in an awkward stage, or they may be trying to process a trusted leader's poor decisions.

6. They may be in bondage to Satan's lies.

7. They may be trying other belief systems to validate their own.

8. They may be rebelling against the flawed brand of Christianity they see.

I (Jill) was a teenager who rebelled. Raised in a moral, churchgoing family, I found the world's ways far too tempting. I knew the basics of right living, but I didn't have a strong enough personal relationship with Jesus Christ to make the right decisions. I was adept at living a double life. My parents were somewhat unaware of the marijuana, alcohol, and promiscuity that surrounded me every day at school. Nor did they know the depth of my involvement.

As a result of my experience, I look beyond what my teenagers say. If they ask to go to someone's house, I don't assume that parents are home—I either ask or call the parents myself. If they ask to spend the night at someone's home, I confirm that the parents will be there. I try to avoid being naive on one hand or suspicious on the other. Rebellious teens need to know that someone cares enough to ask the tough questions and follow up. They also need to know that they are loved unconditionally, regardless of the choices they make.

Calling In Help

Recently our (the Savages') daughter showed us a friend's screen name. It referred to cutting herself. Mark and I would want someone to let us know if our daughter had used that name, so we contacted her parents. The parents knew their daughter struggled emotionally but not to the extent of cutting herself. They now realized their daughter was becoming self-destructive, and they needed to seek professional help for her.

One of our teens struggled with severe emotional lows for several years. We initially thought this was normal for a teenage girl. But eventually we decided to have her talk with a counselor, who suggested a low dose of antidepressant and antianxiety medication for a short season. At first we balked at the idea of medication, but we decided to give it a try. She was amazed at the change in her perspective. Suddenly she could make decisions without falling apart. She could once again socialize with her friends and not be so easily irritated. Her pessimism changed to optimism. I don't believe medication is always the answer, but we should not hesitate to get help for a child who is struggling.

Repairing the Wounded Heart

We (the Farrels) served in a church where a man with several children came out of the closet and marched in a gay pride parade. Not surprisingly, each of the kids struggled with their own faith. We assigned each teen a leader to walk with him or her, but it took years of hard work to walk them through to a stable faith.

Sometimes hard life circumstances can cause a child to struggle with his or her faith. Prepare your kids for the reality of suffering. Teens see a world of AIDS, rape, crime, drugs, violence, famine, and war, and they struggle to make sense of a world in so much pain. Teens with a melancholy personality are prone to look at life at a much deeper level. They may try to carry more of the pain of their world than their young heart can handle. Teens must learn how to trust God through the pain and allow Him to carry its weight.

Right before one of the Farrel boys' senior year, a handful of people in authority positions hurt and disappointed him. He was in pain and confused. I prayed God would show me how to talk with our son. I started the conversation like this:

"Honey, how are you doing with all this? Do you have any questions?"

I answered his questions as honestly yet positively as possible. I tried to explain that everyone is imperfect and in need of God's grace and mercy, and adults in leadership make imperfect decisions. I also warned him that those who hurt us may never apologize or make restitution for what they have done because they may never see things from the same perspective as we do. We talked about what forgiveness is and isn't and reviewed our six statements of forgiveness:

1. I forgive _____ (name the person) for _____ (name the offense).
2. I admit that what happened was wrong.
3. I do not expect _____ (name the person) to make up for what he or she has done.
4. I will not use the offense to define who the person is.
5. I will not manipulate the person with this offense.
6. I will not allow what has happened to stop my personal growth.

Reconciliation: Can We Work It Out?

I looked with my son at Matthew 18, where Jesus shows us how to handle some conflicts. We are to take the initiative and go to an offending person individually. If that meeting is not successful, we should take another person and try again. If we still meet with no response, we are to "tell it to the church" (often those Christians who are closest to the person and may have influence).

"What if you do all those steps and they still don't think what they did was wrong and they still don't care that they hurt you?"

My son's question was a good one. Scripture provides us with some options.

1. Don't throw your pearls before swine. Jesus isn't calling anyone pigs! Rather, if your attempts at reconciliation

are causing more hurt, don't spend yourself unwisely. Your heart is precious, and God doesn't want it discarded.

2. Turn the other cheek. Forgive and move on.

3. Bless them. Give them your coat if they take your cloak. The Bible encourages us to overcome evil with good.

4. Create space. One last option is to treat the person with the same courtesy you show anyone else. A close relationship may not be an option, but you can agree to release one another and be civil.

People rarely intend to hurt us, so we can often forgive them without even talking it out. In some other situations, we can take the next step and talk together honestly. As Steven Covey says, we should seek first to understand and then seek to be understood—ask questions and listen carefully.

Rescuing Faith

Our son was tempted to wonder, is God really good? When we try to do what is right and still suffer abuse, we might feel as if God is being unfair. Watching our children endure unnecessary pain is difficult, so we must guard our own hearts and remain free from bitterness so we can help our kids.

We know that God is good even when people are not good. God is good even when circumstances are not good. God is always good. He has promised to provide us with "hope and a future" (Jeremiah 29:11). We can make a commitment to look for God's goodness and the good path He has for us.

My son and I had many conversations over many months. I hunted down every verse I could about God's goodness, God honoring those who honor Him, and God's anointing and favor. I placed the verses on his pillow and mentioned them in prayer for him. I became vigilant at pointing out signs of God's goodness to our family. I began to pray, "God, send postcards of Your goodness today." Then I'd watch for something that was positive and point it out when I was with my family. I prayed, "God, I need a Post-it note of Your goodness," and God led me to quotes, stories, and verses pointing to the goodness of God and His ability to work out everything for our good.

In the end, God showed His goodness. My son won a college scholarship. Many people came to his graduation party and gave gifts of support and encouragement. One family gave him a laptop computer! He was in awe that so many people would be so good to him!

Some kids' poor decisions are not caused by pain inflicted by others but by their own inner pain. Regardless of how strong-willed your child is, God is stronger still. When you are dealing with a prodigal or a child in emotional pain, you can safeguard your child's future by investing in your own relationship with God. God can hold you up as you hold up your teenager. God will give you what you need when you need it for your child. We moms need to remember that we are not our children's savior—God is. We have seen God strengthen moms as they ministered to kids who were admitted to psychiatric hospitals, kids who suffered through one broken relationship after another, kids who were addicted to drugs and alcohol, and kids who seemed to reject their parents' love.

Tips for Creating Support Teams

Develop a support team for you and another one for your teen. Giving tough love can be excruciatingly painful for a parent. You will need support as you make tough choices. One mom of a prodigal said, "We took our cues from the story of the father of the prodigal in the Bible. He didn't go after his rebelling son but went on with life. He had the family business to run and other children to care for. We did too."

Your Own Team

Select friends who are able to keep confidences, people of prayer and of the same gender who are willing to invest time with you. They do not do the legwork or make calls to gather information for your teen; those are healthy and necessary steps for you to take to stay emotionally strong and connected to your teen. The support team is there to pray and listen. They may offer alternative ideas or help with practical responsibilities. Keep your expectations realistic—these friends have their own lives and responsibilities too. Get your team in place first and then establish your teen's support team.

For Your Teen

Your child's team should be composed of paid professionals as well as lay youth workers and trusted adult family friends. You might include a few young friends if they are mature enough spiritually and emotionally to offer strength and help to your teen.

One mom of a prodigal shared that the turning points in her own daughter's life came when people loved her daughter unconditionally. The daughter's rebellion had led to a traffic accident for which she was responsible. When she was in the hospital, her church family visited her, prayed with her, and brought Christian CDs. When she was released from the hospital and was in court proceedings, her church family continued to love and care for her. When she came to church in short skirts, smoking in the parking lot before and after the services, they continued to love her regardless of what she said or how she acted. One friend took a special interest in the prodigal and met with her weekly, helping her reestablish her relationship with God. Her own parents stood by her but did not rescue her from the consequences of her choices. She is now in jail because of her choices, but her support system continues to love her and reach out to her through the prison walls. She is no longer a prodigal—her heart has softened, and she is walking with God.

 ## *From the Heart*

Watching one of her children hurt is one of the hardest things a mom can do. We can feel helpless when our kids experience disappointment from life circumstances, pain from the consequences of a poor choice, or emotional woundedness from the careless actions of a friend or loved one.

When our children are small, we can kiss their hurts and make them go away. But when our kids enter the teen years, the hurts can't be merely kissed away. Teens have to experience the pain. They have to feel the emotions. They have to learn about the choice of forgiveness firsthand. For a mom, this is one of the hardest parts of letting go and letting your child grow up.

Our role changes when our kids become teenagers. We listen, we encourage, and we share perspective. As God's truth has become our foundation, we can help our teens find their own perspective and comfort from God's Word. God's truth will carry them their entire lives if they will allow it to.

Recently when one of my teens experienced disappointment and betrayal in a friendship, I assured her that Jesus understood her feelings. I explained that Jesus' disciples often let Him down. I reminded her that Jesus understands her hurt, so she can pour out her heart to Him and use this as a time to strengthen her relationship with a God who understands. Don't give up hope—moms can't heal, but we can introduce our children to the Healer!

The Next Step

For you to shepherd your troubled child's heart, you will need to allow God to shepherd your own heart. So what do you do when your own heart is breaking? Here

are six tried-and-true tips that have helped move me
(Pam) forward when I wanted the world to just go away
and leave me alone!

1. *Turn up the truth.* Take in more truth than you
    are giving out. Listen to the Bible on CD and
    praise CDs. Attend a Bible study. Read
    inspiring books. Try reading a new translation
    or paraphrase of the Bible.

2. *Focus forward.* A family friend says, "Life is too
    short to live looking in the rearview mirror." Post
    your long-range goals where you will see them
    often. Display pictures of your family wherever
    you spend the most time. Organize your prayer
    life. Write and frame personal and family mis-
    sion statements. Keep first things first, and don't
    let pain sweep away all that God has given and
    will give.

3. *Research for results.* Any crisis is easier to handle
    with more resources to draw on and more infor-
    mation to use when making crucial decisions.
    Find books by authors who have experienced
    similar situations. Ask a mentor or a trusted
    leader for the names of people who might know
    some information that would help you.

4. *Go on a God hunt.* Look for God to speak every
    day. Look for the good in any situation and notice
    how God works.

5. *Call in the troops.* Some situations are so tough
    that you'll need to call on friends and family to
    rally around you to protect your family, your

faith, and your future. Ask those you love to help you with specific tasks.

6. *Pray in partnership.* Don't endure your pain alone! Get together with a trusted friend for a prayer walk. Make a regular appointment to pray together. Send each other Scriptures of encouragement and plan fun outings to keep perspective and to replenish your heart.

Moms In Touch provides a prayer sheet for moms of prodigals to use to pray for their children in need:

31 Ways to Pray for our Youth

Pray for a spirit of reverence—the fear of the Lord (Proverbs 9:10).

Pray for a spirit of humility—a willingness to submit (Ephesians 4:2).

Pray for a spirit of purity—a desire to be clean (Matthew 5:8).

Pray for a spirit of purpose—the wisdom to set goals (Proverbs 4:25-27).

Pray for a spirit of simplicity—a lifestyle uncluttered (1 Corinthians 14:40).

Pray for a spirit of commitment—a dedication to the cause (Joshua 24:15).

Pray for a spirit of diligence—a willingness to work hard (Colossians 3:23).

Pray for a spirit of servanthood—a willingness to help others (Galatians 6:9-10).

Pray for a spirit of constancy—the quality of faithfulness (Psalm 119:33).

Pray for a spirit of assurance—a depth of faith (1 John 5:13).

Pray for a spirit of availability—a readiness to go (Isaiah 6:8).

Pray for a spirit of loyalty—a zeal for fidelity (Ruth 1:16).

Pray for a spirit of discernment—a perception of wrong (Colossians 2:8).

Pray for a spirit of compassion—love in action (Colossians 3:12).

Pray for a spirit of thankfulness—a heart of gratitude (Colossians 3:17).

Pray for a spirit of maturity—the capacity to grow (Hebrews 5:14).

Pray for a spirit of holiness—Christlike behavior (Acts 24:16).

Pray for a spirit of reliability—a depth of dependability (1 Corinthians 4:2).

Pray for a spirit of revelation—to know God better (Ephesians 1:17).

Pray for a spirit of self-denial—a sacrifice to surrender (Luke 9:23).

Pray for a spirit of confidence—an assurance of competence (Philippians 4:13).

Pray for a spirit of integrity—the quality of uprightness (Romans 12:17).

Pray for a spirit of repentance—a willingness to change (Ezekiel 18:30-31).

Pray for a spirit of trust—a steadfast belief (Psalm 125:1).

Pray for a spirit of submission—choosing to yield (1 Peter 2:13-14,17).

Pray for a spirit of teachability—learning from others (Proverbs 6:20).

Pray for a spirit of prayer—being persistent (Luke 18:1).

Pray for a spirit of unity—a respect for others (Psalm 133:1).

Pray for a spirit of truthfulness—delighting in honesty (Proverbs 12:22).

Pray for a spirit of forgiveness—an ability to show grace (Ephesians 4:32).

Pray for a spirit of generosity—the desire to give (Hebrews 13:16).[2]

A Mom's Prayer

Lord, give me wisdom as I help my teens through their choices. Help me not to react but to realize that rebellion may be caused by emotional pain, questions, or a strong will. Give me the support I need to give my teens the support they need. Pull us through this time and set our feet on You, our Rock and Salvation. Amen.

A Pastor at Home

Impacting Children Spiritually so They Will Have an Impact

The way into a church for a tween, teen or college student is not the front door but the *back door*. For someone older than 11, church is usually all about relationships. Kids care about theology, but *people* taught them that theology, and *people* will teach them even more life lessons ahead. You may have learned from personal experience that *people* are often the hands and feet of God.

Still, the Person you most want teaching your kids is a *personal* God! Your goal is to help your students have a vibrant, relevant, *personal* relationship with God. That connection will help your teens make wise choices now, and it will provide a stable foundation as they spread their wings and fly.

How can a mom foster healthy relationships in her kids' lives? When does "providing opportunities" turn into pushiness or control? How can you find people who care about your children's spiritual growth? How do you create an environment where those relationships can lead to positive, life-changing experiences? How can you connect your child or young adult to relationships that will move them closer to God?

The Youth Pastor, Your New Best Friend

If you are not attending a church where there is an active youth ministry, you might want to consider making a change. The positive investment that a strong youth program can make in the life of a teen is incredibly important in this formative, peer-pressure-filled season of life. If you are attending a church with an active youth ministry, connect with the youth leaders in a personal way. You need them in your child's life.

What are some ways to build bridges between your child, your family, and the youth pastor or youth staff?

- *Be interested.* Register early for events. Volunteer to contact other parents.
- *Be on the team.* Ask what you can do to help. (Ask your son or daughter first to make sure he or she is comfortable with you volunteering in this way.)
- *Be a friend.* Try to make the youth pastor's life a little easier. Most youth pastors have a pretty limited salary, so coupons for movies, meals, or car repair go a long way in showing appreciation.
- *Be alert.* You might know the inside scoop on happenings at the local public school, in the neighborhood, or in the family of a problem child.
- *Be prayerful.* Youth work is a battle zone. Pray for the youth pastor, his staff, and his family.

- *Be assertive.* If you are new to a church, invite the youth pastor and his family over for a meal, or offer to pay for him to take your child out for a soda or burger.
- *Be encouraging.* If your kids have ministry gifts that can build up the church, encourage them to use them. Encourage them to serve musically or assist in Sunday school.
- *Be an investigator.* As your college student moves away to school, you might have to help your student find churches, mentors, and on-campus groups.

Other Spiritual Mentors

We want our teenagers to be surrounded by many adults who will steer them in the right direction. We want our kids to know of several people they could call if they were in a quandary.

We (the Farrels) have always encouraged teens to be involved in several groups that would help them grow in their relationship with Christ. We wanted to expose the kids to a broad range of spiritual opportunities so they could make wise, informed choices about their own spiritual personality, worship likes, and teaching style. Our kids were exposed to the traditional hymns of the faith and the calm experience of rituals (like communion, baptism, congregational readings, and candlelight services). They were also given opportunities to be a part of a much more experiential worship experience—one that was sometimes louder than my ears are comfortable with! They were a part of a group that made sharing their faith a priority, another that made Bible study a priority, and still another that provided a fun, safe, and relevant place for them to bring their unchurched, pre-believing friends. These are a few parachurch groups you might want to investigate:

College and High School Campus Ministries

InterVarsity (www.intervarsity.org) instills a love for studying the Bible and provides an intellectual defense of the faith. They also host Urbana, a huge missions expo, every two years. InterVarsity serves more than 35,000 students and faculty on more than 560 college and university campuses nationwide.

Navigators (www.navigators.org) specializes in one-to-one discipleship and leadership training. They offer Nav U, small- and large-group Bible studies, and summer leadership training programs. Their college ministry is just one of many facets of a growing organization (including Glen Eyrie conference center and NavPress). Dawson Trotman started Navigators in 1933 as a Sunday school class of high schoolers.

Chi Alpha (www.chialpha.com) dates back to the late 1940s when J. Robert Ashcroft, the father of former U.S. Attorney General John Ashcroft, began encouraging the General Council of the Assemblies of God to start a ministry that would reach beyond the church walls to students on secular college campuses. Students at Southwest Missouri State University who were already meeting informally put the idea into practice and launched the first official Chi Alpha chapter in 1953. Chi Alpha has grown to over 200 groups here in the U.S. Chi Alpha derives its name from the first two letters of the Greek words *Christou Apostoloi*—Christ's Ambassadors.

Campus Crusade for Christ (www.ccci.org) was started in 1959 by Bill and Vonette Bright with the goal of reaching college campuses with the good news of a personal relationship with Christ. Today it is on 1029 college campuses. Student Venture, the junior high and high school ministry, started in 1966 and now has 1300 staff workers.

Young Life (www.younglife.org) is a lively parachurch outreach that hosts fun events for the purpose of presenting Christianity in a nonthreatening way. They offer *Young Life Magazine,* which is a healthy alternative to today's teen pop culture tabloids. Young Life began in 1941 and now is active in all 50 states and more than 45 countries, reaching an estimated one million teenagers annually. More than 90,000 kids spend a weekend during the school year or a week during the summer at one of Young Life's 24 camping properties in the United States and Canada.

Fellowship of Christian Athletes (www.fca.org) was started by a group of professional athletes, businessmen, and coaches. The vision of FCA is "to present to athletes and coaches and all whom they influence the challenge and adventure of receiving Jesus Christ as Savior and Lord, serving Him in their relationships and in the fellowship of the church." FCA offers summer camps taught by college and professional coaches. The camp "huddles" are lead by college athletes who love Christ.

Youth for Christ International (www.yfci.org) began in the 1940s with a vision to reach out to young people who weren't responding to traditional church ministries. Its high school outreach is called Campus Life. YFC's first full-time worker was the young Billy Graham. More than 4500 full- and part-time staff now serve in more than 100 countries.

Missions Organizations

Athletes of Good News (www.aogn.org) is a national organization that recognizes outstanding Christian Athletes and offers SportsQuest, a summer mission trip for athletes.

Youth with a Mission (www.ywamfm.org) is one of the largest missions organizations that offers opportunities for kids. It was founded in 1960 and has about 12,000 volunteer staff (and thousands more affiliated workers) in more than 135 countries.

Real Impact Missions (www.realimpact.com) functions in 150 countries and offers personalized missions trips.

The Continentals and Young Continentals (www.continental singers.org) offer music, dance, and drama ministry opportunities in the U.S. and abroad.

Your own denomination is a great place to find a missions adventure. By teaming with your denomination, you partner with your local church to further its mission. You may be able to go on a missions trip as a family, building shared memories and helping you to connect with your child's friendship circle. Your child could also go year after year and build long-term relationships with missionaries and the local people he or she serves.

Digging In for Themselves

We moms are our children's first teacher. Often we are the catalyst for connecting our kids with God, but we want to work our way out of being the go-between in this relationship. We want our teens to own their own relationship with God. One way to encourage this is to help your teen establish a daily quiet time or devotional time when he or she prays, reads the Bible, and maybe writes in a journal. Take your teen to a local Christian bookstore and ask the salesperson to show your teen a variety of teen devotional books and Bibles.

You will also want to teach your teens to study the Bible for themselves. Get them a Bible they understand (many newer translations are available) and a journal or notebook, and then teach them how to pull out information and applications from the Bible they can use in their daily life. Here are a few simple ways to dig in to the Word of God:

A, E, I, O, U

A friend of mine shared a simple system she learned from the Navigators. It's as easy as saying your vowels.

A—Ask questions. Read a passage and try to come up with ten questions to ask of the text.

E—Emphasize. Find definitions for key words; look up meaning of key phrases. (You will need a dictionary, a Bible dictionary, and maybe a Bible encyclopedia.)

I—In your own words. Write a paraphrase of a passage in your own words.

O—Other references. Use cross-references to lead you to other verses and consult commentaries.

U—You! Choose a personal application. The sooner you can apply the verse the better!

Character Study

Encourage your student to read the Bible and study the lives of the people in it. For example, girls might enjoy reading the books of Ruth and Esther. Guys might want to look up passages that talk about men like David, Paul, Abraham, Joshua, or Daniel. Have your teens make two columns in their journal: Things This Person Did Right and Things This Person Did Wrong. At the bottom of the page, have them explain how this applies to their own life.

A Psalm and a Chapter in Proverbs a Day Helps to Keep the Devil Away

Encourage your student to read a chapter in Proverbs a day or a Psalm a day. (Because there are 31 chapters in Proverbs, your teen can read a chapter a day for each corresponding day of the month.) Have him or her write a love letter to God in response to what they read. Creative teens might choose to write a song or poem in response.

Question It

A fun way to go deeper is to "dialogue" with the word of God.

Ask God questions about what you read. If you can access Biblegate
way.com, you can print out entire sections of Scripture and search
online reference works for answers. Below is a small sample of questions to ask:

> *Who* wrote it and to whom?
>
> *What* is the context of this story (What is going on before
> and after this passage)?
>
> *When* did it take place in history? What do I need to know
> about the author's culture?
>
> *Where* did the author and his readers live? Where are the
> geographic areas that the text mentions? (Have a book
> of Bible maps handy.)
>
> *Why* did the author write this? Is this a teaching passage?
> A poem that shares feeling? A story that illustrates a
> point?
>
> *How* does this apply to life today? To my life?

(For more information on this method of study and other ways
to study the Bible, read *How to Study Your Bible* by Kay Arthur or *Living
by the Book* by Howard Hendricks.)

1, 2, 3

I learned three simple questions as an 18-year-old college student
that launched me into the Bible daily.

1. *What does it say?* What are the facts? What's going on
   in the story of passage?

2. *What does it mean?* Do I understand the meaning, or
   do I need to look up the meaning of some words? Do

I need to cross-reference some other verses to see what else the Bible says about this topic? Do I need to investigate the culture, review some history, or read a commentary?

3. *What does it mean to me?* How can I apply it today to my life? What do I do with this new information?

As you can see, your students have many ways they can dig into the Bible for themselves. Reward them when they do. We (the Farrels) always reward spiritual growth with more opportunities for spiritual growth. For example, when our kids were first learning how to have a daily quiet time, I asked them to complete some Bible study books. When they completed a book, they could select a new Christian music CD at the bookstore. If they are older and the devotional is longer, offer to pay their way to a Christian camp or concert. By the time they are in college, studying the Bible for what it can do for their lives and for what they gain in the relationship with God should be its own reward. I began weaning our kids off external awards at about 16 or 17 as they started choosing how they wanted to study the Bible and selecting their own devotional material.

They Are Watching You

To raise a child who hungers for God, you must model a desire to know and please God. If you treat your relationship with God casually, that's the attitude your children will pick up too. Do they see and hear you pray? Read your Bible? Sing worship songs outside of church? Share your faith with friend? Serve your community? Do they see you go out of your way to grow with God? I want my kids to see a mom always growing in her faith in God. As your teens mature, you will want to stay at least a step ahead of them spiritually by investing in your own walk with God.

Our children need to see us search out God's Word for our life. They need to see us look for truth and apply it to our life and actions. As a teenager, I (Jill) chose a life of promiscuity. I remember when my parent's found out that I was sexually active. It was a difficult season for my parents and me. I particularly remember one conversation my mother and I had that went like this:

Mom: "Sex outside of marriage is wrong."

Me: "How do you know it's wrong?"

Mom: "The Bible says it's wrong."

Me: "If the Bible is so important for my life, why don't I see you using it for your life?"

My family was a moral, churchgoing family, but I had only seen either of my parents opening the Bible if they had a Sunday school lesson to teach. I had never seen them open God's Word for their own life. I had never seen their hearts turned by God's truth. That didn't mean it hadn't happened, but I hadn't witnessed it, and they had never openly shared with me about the effect of God's truth on their heart.

I have never forgotten that season of my life. Instead of being frustrated when my children interrupt my quiet time with God, I'm thankful they can see me searching out truth. When I'm convicted by God's truth, I try to remember to share what God is teaching me with my teens so they know that truth is life-changing at every age and stage in life.

Teens can spot a hypocrite a mile away. As parents, we have to walk the talk and live the life we want our children to live as well.

One mom I know had a creative way to encourage her two teenage sons to have quiet times. She found it easier to have her quiet time away from the distractions at home, so each weekday morning she would get up and go to a restaurant to have her time with God. She invited the boys to join her at the restaurant before school and offered to buy their breakfast if they came and brought their Bible and a journal. The boys and their mom made this their morning routine throughout their high school years, and now those boys are grown with families of their own. They are godly men who are grounded in their relationship with the Lord. Their mom's creativity helped set a foundation for their lives.

 ### *From the Heart*

I was raised with a foundation of faith, but I never really understood a personal relationship with Jesus Christ until my adult years. As a mother, I wanted to give my children a foundation of faith, but I wanted to do even more than that. I wanted to introduce them to a relevant, living, daily friendship with God. And in order to do that, I had to venture into new ground. I had to take some risks. I had to have some interactions with my kids that I had not had modeled in my own life. God was really stretching me!

When I was growing up, we prayed at meals and at bedtime. But as an adult I was learning to "practice the presence of God" all day long. I came to trust God not only as my Savior but as Lord of my life, talking to Him all day. I wanted my kids to be able to do the same. The first time one of them asked a question that I didn't know how to answer, I had to say, "I don't know what to tell you about that, but what I do know is that God has the answer. Let's pray and ask God for His direction and wisdom." And then we did just that. We prayed in the middle of our kitchen at 3:30 in the afternoon! I'd never seen that done, and it did feel a little odd, but I pushed through the uncomfortable feeling and took a step of leadership for my child. Now, many years later, it's very common for Mark or me to pray with our kids for just about anything. Just yesterday I was shopping at the mall when my cell phone rang. Our daughter in college was on the other end of the line in tears. I listened as she shared some disappointments she was experiencing as well as some fears about future decisions. After she and I discussed some strategies for processing her struggles I said, "Let me pray for you, Anne." And there I stood, just outside of Bath and Body Works, praying over the phone with my then 19-year-old daughter!

You will want to do some things differently from the way you were raised, and they will initially feel uncomfortable for you. But once you take the first step, the second time is a little easier, and the third time still easier. Eventually the new way of doing things becomes a part of the fabric of your family, and you are on your way to being a mom who intentionally shares Christ with her teens.

The Next Step

Where do you need to begin?

1. *With yourself.* Learn how to spend time with God first. Perhaps you know how to spend time with God but are in a rut, have a bad attitude about spiritual growth, or have been lazy lately. What adjustments do you want to make in order to be a better role model for your teenager?

2. *With a youth pastor.* Look for one or make an appointment with the one you have and see how you might help him or her.

3. *With some tools.* Equip your teen with some devotional books or journals.

   • Sit with your teen and try some of the ideas in this chapter on ways to spend time with God.

- Set aside time to pray with your child or pray for your child. The Farrels and Savages like to do both. We pray with our kids on the way out the door, on the phone, over meals, and at bedtime. I (Jill) like to kneel next to each of my children's beds to pray for them specifically after they leave for school. I (Pam) also pray for my kids each week at a Moms In Touch meeting with other moms. And my husband and I have a regular time of prayer for them each night at bedtime. I also walk and swim, and I make praying for my kids a part of my daily exercise routine too.

A Mom's Prayer

Lord, help me have a vital connection with You, and give me creativity to help my teens develop their own connection to You. Amen.

The Social Activist

Creating Citizens Who Are World Changers

The first time I (Pam) met Sean, he was about eight years old. He showed up in Sunday school in perfectly pressed khakis, a clean white shirt, and a tie. He sat up straight in his chair, he didn't fidget, and his hand was the first one up to answer every question. I was so impressed with him that I went home that day and told Bill, "I'm really looking forward to meeting the Harringtons—the new family who visited church today. Their son, Sean, was in my class, and if he were running for political office today, I'd vote for him! I might even be his campaign manager!" He's now 17 and I still feel that way. He is already an outstanding young leader and a catalyst for social change.

And the apple doesn't fall far from the tree. I mentored his mother, Penny, through some Bible studies. Actually, I learned more from her than she did from me. She is who I go to when I need an opinion I can trust. She is a mom with her ear to the ground, and she knows what is happening in the world around us. She's on a mission to help make the world a safer place for children and grandchildren to grow up in.

Penny and I have linked arms. My message to women all over the world for years has been this: One ordinary woman connected to the extraordinary God can make a difference. Penny often tells moms where and how they can make such a difference. Together, we have committed to help moms avoid maternal myopia—seeing only the needs of their own children while missing what is going on in the world around them. I asked Penny how we can help teens become active, involved citizens.

Penny, you are very active in Concerned Women for America (CWA). How has that helped you as a mother?

CWA provides a lot of information that none of us would be aware of if we relied solely on the mainstream media. Organizations such as CWA offer insights into policies, legislation, and events occurring in education and family policy that help parents be more effective in their schools and in their children's lives.

How can a mom raise children who care about social issues?

Of course, we need to educate our children at an age-appropriate level about the threats to our faith and our families. We must help them develop a worldview so that God's Word, rather than their peers or the media, guides their thinking about culture. Beyond knowing why they believe what they believe, however, children need to see our faith in action. If we are to be the good examples the Bible calls us to be, we need to be participants in the public arena. We can take our kids with us when we donate time or goods to the homeless shelter or when we attend a Walk for Life or other public demonstration of our convictions. We can hardly grumble and complain about the plight if we're not willing to be part of the fight!

How can teens take a stand on social issues?

Many public policy groups have incredible resources on their websites to help students:

- Alliance Defense Fund (www.alliancealert.org)
- Concerned Women for America (www.cwfa.org)
- Reclaiming America (www.reclaimingamerica.org)

- Focus on Social Issues (www.family.org/cforum/fosi)

Also, family-friendly thinkers abound at townhall.com.

How can we help teens become more interested in social issues?

Since interest has to come from inside, this one is tougher. Parents are key here. Older children can be very helpful in local political campaigns by making signs, stuffing envelopes, or walking precincts (with an adult, of course!). Youth groups and clubs can encourage, hands-on compassion by organizing missions trips, whether to Mexico or to a local homeless shelter. Serving helps kids think outside themselves. *World Magazine,* an excellent news magazine for Christian adults, also has a kids' version *(God's World News)* for home or school subscriptions. Some articles are available online at www.gwnews.com.

How can moms help their college students maintain their faith and beliefs as they enter college?

Having a strong Christian worldview going into college (particularly to a public school) is extremely important. It's hard to break down a solid foundation. To help prepare a student for the onslaught of liberal thinking from peers and professors, Focus on the Family has developed *Boundless Webzine* (www.boundless.org). The site encourages young adults to think with a faith mind-set. Dr. J. Budziszewski's *How to Stay Christian in College* is a great tool for those heading off to school.

What resources are available for college students interested in social justice?

 All the sites I've mentioned have great resources for politics and social issues. A college student also has opportunities for internships at many of the public policy organizations in Washington, D.C. Even state public policy groups often have special days for students—high school and college. Concerned Women for America, Family Research Council, Capitol Resource Institute (in California), and others are very receptive to internships. Most colleges can help students search for these connections, or they can be contacted through their websites.

What is one decision you made that has helped Sean become such a strong leader?

Steve and I believe we made two important decisions for our boys. The first was the choice for me to stay at home. When our oldest was four, we tightened our belts and I left my career. I volunteered at their schools, became involved in helping others, and delved into my passion, which was public policy. There is really no substitute for one-on-one time with our children, and it's the only way to instill our core values in them. No one can raise your children better than you can.

We were blessed with great teachers in our local public school until fifth grade. They had all demonstrated strong teaching skills and a conservative philosophy. At fifth grade, however, we could not find a good choice for our son. We felt God leading us, instead, to a wonderful Christian school. There he grew academically and spiritually. He was mentored by strong Christian men and women who helped us encourage his leadership ability. When he entered high school, he returned to a public school campus as a leader, not a follower.

I am in no way denigrating public schools, however. Some wonderful Christian men and women teach there, and children can benefit from their mentorship. However, parents must be involved in the public schools, not only in the classrooms but also in administration and district policies.

How can we protect our children?

Vigilance is the watchword for our children in our culture. No home should be without an Internet filter. The average age of addiction to pornography gets younger each year. With unfiltered Internet access, nearly every child will be exposed to porn. We must protect our children in every way possible, and you can protect them online for pennies a day without slowing down your server. Visit www.filterreview.com to check out your options. We use Bsafe Online (www.afafilter.com).

Another important concern is movies. Several sites help parents make decisions about what movies their children (or they themselves!) should see. We can't trust PG or PG-13 ratings anymore. Get the facts. Visit www.screenit.com or www.pluggedinonline.com for thorough reviews.

In school, we need to take our rightful place as parents. Pacific Justice Institute has helpful books and brochures at www.pacificjustice.org/resources/bookbroch/. The most important thing we can do is talk to our children. Ask every day what happened at school. Volunteer to work in the classroom or on the school site. Attend school board meetings and know who your board members are. Get other parents involved too. Watch and listen.

Also, check out the sex education curriculum. You have the right to ask for all the books, materials, and notes the presenters will use. If you are not happy with everything that is to be presented, opt your child out. If you think they'll feel uncomfortable being the only one, get other parents to do the same. The homosexual viewpoint has infiltrated our schools to a greater and greater degree. Sex ed is not the only curricula affected, so be very vigilant and in an age-appropriate way equip your child with the facts about the emotional and physical danger of this behavior.

Join a Moms In Touch prayer group for your child's school. Nothing beats prayer! (www.momsintouch.org).

How can moms stay better informed about public policy issues?

Another helpful resource regarding the media and culture for parents is the American Family Association (www.afa.net). They are a media watchdog for families. Through their alert system and easy steps, you can make your voice heard on everything from sleazy television shows to trashy corporate tactics.

How can we as moms be alert and aware without becoming overprotective or paranoid?

If we're well informed, we have no reason to be paranoid. We have the facts, and the answer is not fear but focus. We could lose this generation if we don't step up.

It's hard to imagine being overprotective in this culture, but we do have to let children fight their own battles as they are able. That's where our equipping is so important. We must help build that rock-solid foundation so they will make wise choices and we won't have to smother them as they get older.

If you had one word of advice for mothers, what would it be?

You can't get more articulate than God: "Train up a child in the way he should go, and when he is old he will not turn from it" (Proverbs 22:6). This is not a promise that our efforts will always result in perfect children leading perfect lives. Rather, it means they will not be able to run from the foundational truth you've given them.

Be First!

One of my (Pam's) goals as a mother was to be the first to teach my child about topics like sexuality and public policy. This meant as Brock moved from stage to stage, I took time to quiz other moms who had children one or two years older than mine. I asked them what issues they faced in the schools in the past few years. I asked if they were working on any policies or trying to navigate any positive changes that I could help with. By asking these questions, I learned of some important issues ahead of time. That enabled me to educate myself and find tools to better educate my kids.

Hunt Down Help!

Bill and I also made some goals for our sons, and then I went to work hunting down options to use to help us meet those goals. For example, I wanted children who had a Christian worldview, who could accurately articulate their faith. When they were little and had to study dinosaurs, I got them picture books from Institute for Creation Research. When they were older, I went back to ICR for more grown-up creationist resources. I found other organizations to help prepare my sons articulate their belief in God, the Bible, and matters of faith related to daily living.

A variety of videos are available, including Josh McDowell's Truth Matters Video Series (based on his book *Right from Wrong*),

WallBuilders' videos on the Christian history of our country, and R.C. Sproul's *Choosing My Religion.*

Wisdom from Insiders and the Internet

We moms want to be in the know about the newest trends and terrors. Focus on the Family offers three top-notch magazines: *Brio* for girls, *Breakaway* for boys, and *Plugged In* for parents and other adults who work with kids. These are wholesome magazines that reinforce traditional family values, encourage spiritual growth, and hold up positive Christian role models. The Savage family has found *Plugged In* to be very valuable in helping us understand the media culture in which we live. When *Plugged In* arrives in our home, our teenagers rush to be the first to read it. They soak up the articles that address movies, music, and television shows. Mark and I have found both the magazine and www.pluggedinonline.com to be very helpful in understanding our teenagers' world.

The Barna Group (www.barna.org) is another helpful resource. George Barna keeps his thumb on the pulse of the nation. Early trends will usually first be seen by this statistician and researcher.

Get in the Game

The best way to prepare teens for battle is to go into battle with them. As a family, participate in Walks for Life or pro-life or pro-marriage rallies. Campaign together for a candidate who represents Christian values. Offer your home as an alternative to wild prom parties by hosting your own nonalcoholic event. Look for the challenges that trip kids up, and offer options that are smarter and more fun. Your teens will always find themselves with a strong set of peers to hang out with.

For a season, Mark and I have set aside our visions of quiet evenings on the weekends. For now, we want our home to be a place where our teenagers want to hang with their friends. I keep snacks in a hiding place so I can pull them out when our teenagers have spontaneous parties. We have a dartboard and Ping-Pong table in the garage and a basketball hoop in the driveway to give the kids something to do together. During the fall we build a bonfire (we live in the country) just about every Friday night where the kids can hang out and talk with their friends.

For homecoming at his public high school, Evan asked if he and a few friends could have dinner at our house. Instead of going to a nice restaurant before the homecoming dance, they wanted a cookout where they could come in casual dress, shoot some baskets, play Ping-Pong, or jump on the trampoline. Then they changed clothes, we took pictures, and off they went to the dance. We initially planned for 12 friends. But the guest list grew, and we hosted 26 kids at the cookout! Several other parents pitched in and helped provide the food. They were glad to have a safe place for their kids to go and have fun.

Address Issues in an Age-Appropriate Way

Regardless of how diligent a parent is, negative influences will come pounding at your door. When Brock was ten, he was in a children's theater production of Tom Sawyer. His Christian school teacher was the director, and most of the cast were kids from the Christian school—but not all. While changing their clothes, I stood in the hallway and heard a junior higher shout, "You queer! You are such a faggot!" Then I heard my son say, "What's that?" I immediately yelled in, "Never mind, Brock. You need to get on stage. We'll answer your question later." I had not even explained heterosexual sex completely to him, so I didn't want some junior higher explaining homosexuality to him! That was a job for his dad and me.

And issues like this cannot be ignored. What do you tell your young children when a relative is gay or in a live-in heterosexual relationship? If an aunt is living with a man and isn't married, a two-year-old isn't going to know the difference, but a tween or teen will. However, kids will ask questions anyway, so you should probably explain the situation beforehand. The conversation might sound like this with a tween:

> Honey, you know Aunt Corrie will be at Christmas this year. She will have her boyfriend, Todd, with her. They are not married yet, but they live in the same house. Aunt Corrie is a very nice person. She loves you very much, but this is one decision she has made that Mom and Dad don't agree with. You don't need to talk to her about it. That is something Mom and Dad will do. Just love her and pray for her. If you want to talk to Todd or play checkers in the living room, that's fine, but you don't have to do anything with Todd you don't want to. Let's just be nice to him, and our family will just call him Todd. We will love him like Jesus loves him, okay?

A child should not be forced to go anywhere alone with a family member or friend, nor should your children feel family pressure to call anyone Aunt or Uncle if they are not. Teens can be given freedom to bring up any topics with relatives if they do it with respect. Dialogue with family can help teens and college students grow stronger in their views.

For example, our sons have grown tremendously because of their relationship with an aunt and an uncle and whose views on social and political subjects are usually opposite of ours. The conversation around the dinner table during their summer visits has been stimulating and honest. We do not want to shelter our kids from reality. Rather, we want to gradually expose them to the realities of life in age-appropriate increments so we can prepare and equip them to share their faith in an unholy world while maintaining their personal holiness.

The homosexual issue is a little more complicated. You may want to just tell your child that Uncle Jerry will have his friend Trent there and leave it at that. If they express public affection in front of your child, privately ask your family member not to do this in front of your young child. If they are unwilling, you are free to leave. If they are in your home, you are free to ask the family member to abide by your wishes in your home. If they are unwilling, you may decide to ask them to leave.

You are the parent. You control much of the environment that surrounds your children, and you are the filter through which the world reaches your teen's heart. Never be embarrassed when you stand up for your child. Your most important relationship is with your kids.

Neutral Ground

Most issues do not require a showdown. If you have extended family members who have values very different from your own, one way to handle the differences is to meet on neutral ground. For example, a family could have a reunion at a tourist spot that offers both wholesome family activities like boating, crafts, and hiking along with evening activities that the rest of your extended family may desire.

We have avoided trouble by initiating extended family get-togethers. If we invite the family to join us at an amusement park or at a Christian family camp, the other family members are free to join us or not. But they know they are loved and that we desire to build a relationship with them.

Keep Your Values

The biggest challenge may come when you are invited to homes that do not share your value system. In these situations, I usually respond by phone and ask if I can help out or bring anything. We tend to go early to these events and leave early because the longer people drink the more their behavior changes.

At these kinds of events, we bow our heads to pray before a meal. In a small setting, we ask if we might bless the food, and we always thank God for the host family and their kind and generous hearts. As the kids hit their teen years, we had a family signal that meant it is time to leave. This prevented arguments as we prepared the family to leave and say our thank-yous and goodbyes.

When do you send a teen into potentially challenging circumstances? Our goal was that by the time our children were 14, they would know how to handle difficult circumstances. For example, one night our 14-year-old wanted to go to a party at a friend's home. A group of freshmen were spending the night, playing video games, and talking sports. We said, "Tell us why we should say yes." Brock made the phone call to his friend to find out the answers to every question we might ask: Would his parents be home? Will there be alcohol? Will older teens attend? When should he come? What will they be doing? When is it over?

After Brock gave us all the right answers, we said, "Sure, go and enjoy—but what's your backup plan in case something goes wrong?"

"I'll call you and you'll come pick me up."

Brock got to his friend's, and everything was fine until some older football players showed up with beer, and the single mom refused to come out and deal with it. The older players wouldn't listen to the freshmen players' request to leave and take their beer with them. Brock called and asked if all the freshman could come hang out at our home instead, and he convinced a few seniors who didn't want to drink to come along as well. He managed to maintain the friendship with his host, keep his integrity, and positively impact others in the process.

We want our sons to grow to the place they can go to a business dinner where other may be drinking yet graciously decide not to. We want them to be gracious guests who over dinner can discuss issues that might lead to the host asking for more information about God.

You win more friends with sugar than vinegar. We want our kids to be positive and proactive. We remember the days when we were the teens living in homes where God was not the center, so we want our kids to befriend unchurched kids and show them the love of God.

When Evil Enters In

How do you handle sin when it comes into your home uninvited? When do you forgo rescuing others to provide safety for your own?

When I was a freshman in high school, my (Jill's) family decided to host a foreign exchange student in our home. Sylvia came to the United States at the young age of 13. She was living with her single mother in Paris but had pretty much raised herself.

Sylvia and I shared a room during our freshman year in high school. Until then, I had lived a pretty sheltered life. Sylvia introduced me to a life I didn't know existed: smoking, drinking, marijuana, and sex before marriage.

My parents were unaware of the temptations Sylvia brought into our home. As a parent, I have tried to not be naive about the influence of friends. I have not hesitated to challenge our kids to make good friendship and relationship choices, and I have pointed out certain behaviors that I see in their friends that concern me.

Boys also have to face the influence of Internet porn. Porn distributors spend millions to find ways around firewalls to hook men young and old. If you discover your son is viewing something on the Internet he should not, here are a few things to keep in mind:

1. *Do not freak out.* Adding shame will not help matters. Satan would love to cause a deeper rift between a son and his parents.

2. *Do not overreact.* Most all men will have to face down this demon at some point in their development. Your

son is not abnormal, sick, or deviant. He is trapped. Help free him by teaming up to offer him the "way out" that 1 Corinthians 10:13 talks about.

3. *Do get him help.* Many good counselors specialize in this common area of struggle. Several good books are available, including *Every Man's Battle* (and *Every Young Man's Battle*). Support groups and mentors are also available.

4. *Do place new boundaries in place.* You may need to change Internet providers or hold a password so you know when your son is surfing the Net. He may also need the accountability of his dad asking him how he is doing. (Uncles, grandfathers, and youth pastors can also be helpful.) Having the computer in a public room (like the living room) can help (when you are at home).

5. *Do applaud him* as he develops new skills to help himself overcome. A young man who has an intense relationship with Christ will have more power to overcome this snare. Applaud your son when he takes appropriate risks, including involvement in missions, evangelism, and pursuing his life's calling. Encourage hobbies that might seem risky to you like whitewater rafting or rock climbing. These might not seem connected, but we have seen that a young man who has a vibrant relationship with Christ and feels he is out on the edge of life pursuing healthy goals doesn't have the time or as much inclination to risk in areas of sin.

Help Them Learn to Think, Not Just Feel

Help your teens consider the long-term consequences of their choices. Josh McDowell made a necklace for his daughter that held three hearts and three question marks. Before every decision, he taught his children to ask, "Does this show love for God? Love for others? Love for myself?"

At a Hearts at Home conference, I picked up a necklace that has three symbols on it that stand for Jesus, Others, and Yourself. I thought it was a great gift for the girls in my extended family because it teaches you will have JOY when your priorities are correct.

If we are going to help kids think and not just feel, we need to help them learn the importance of delaying gratification. Dessert after the dishes are done. Nintendo after they have saved for it. Use of the car when they know how to change the oil and tires. If we give in every time our teens want something, we teach them to think with their eyes: "I want it now, regardless of what I have to do to get it."

This can be a difficult thing for a mother. We want our children to be happy, so we desire to give them nice things. We may also feel some guilt over our own busy schedules, so to express love, we say yes too often and buy them things instead of giving them time. Before you give something, simply ask yourself, *Does my teenager need this?* To ask that question we may have to define *need.*

When They Fall Short

Our teens won't be perfect, so they need to learn how to regroup and recover. Knowing how God would want them to handle sin is just as important as doing the right thing in the first place. 1 John 1:9 says, "If we confess our sins, he is faithful and just and will forgive us our sins and purify us from all unrighteousness." Here are the steps God would like us (and our kids) to take when we fall short.

1. *Acknowledge God is the giver of grace.* "And the LORD said, 'I will cause all my goodness to pass in front of you, and I will proclaim my name, the LORD, in your presence. I will have mercy on whom I will have mercy,

and I will have compassion on whom I will have compassion'" (Exodus 33:19).

2. *Accept God's forgiveness.* Teach your teen to accept the mercy, grace, and forgiveness of God.

3. *Acknowledge your sin.* "He who conceals his sins does not prosper, but whoever confesses and renounces them finds mercy" (Proverbs 28:13). Don't make excuses or rationalize—confess.

4. *Amend your mistakes as much as possible.* If you hurt another, apologize. If you can correct the mistake, do so. If you can make amends, try to restore the relationship.

5. *Actively pursue accountability.* Sin sneaks in. Encourage your teen to be accountable to adults in authority and to their own friends for their choices and behavior.

From the Heart

There is a fine line between protecting our children and sheltering them to a point where they are ill-equipped to live in a fallen world. I've had to learn when to let my children fight their own battles and when to step in and be an advocate for them.

In late elementary school, Evan had two years of less than ideal teachers. His grades were plummeting as quickly as his self-confidence. Mark and I decided that the best strategy for his education would be to homeschool him to assure a positive learning environment and build up his confidence. We needed to be defenders for our son. After two years of homeschooling, Evan reentered the public school system with a fresh vision and a new sense of confidence. He had transformed from a follower into a leader. Our advocacy paid off.

When Anne was a freshman in high school, her world history teacher assigned some extra credit reading that she found offensive.

It was a graphic description of the extramarital affairs and orgies that kings of the fifteenth century had. When Anne showed it to us, we were sickened by the assigned reading. We categorized it as pornographic and very inappropriate for teenagers to be reading. When the teacher dismissed Anne's concerns, we determined the need to step in. The teacher also dismissed our concerns, so we took it to the principal, who negotiated an alternate extra-credit option.

During her senior year in high school, Anne had a lead role in her school musical. Her part called for her to utter a profanity. She was not willing to do so. The director of the musical rebuffed her concerns and told her she needed to follow the script. Mark and I determined that this was a battle Anne needed to fight on her own. With God's help, I exerted every ounce of self-control I could muster to not march into the school and let the director know what I thought. Anne needed to stand on her own principles—the ones that would guide her for a lifetime. She needed to fight for what was right and see the reality of the world she lived in. In the end, Anne made the right moral choice and changed the words she used in the play. The teacher was not happy, but Anne was far more concerned about what God thought than what the teacher who was directing the musical thought.

To be activists for our kids, we need the help of a God who has the wisdom and discernment to handle each situation. When you don't know where to step in and where to back off, ask God for His direction. He'll show you the right steps to take, and He'll make every situation an opportunity for your teen to learn and grow.

The Next Step

How will you get well connected so you are informed and aware? Select several of the resources or websites we've mentioned and keep up on them. For example,

I (Pam) love Concerned Women for America and American Family Association's One Million Moms. In just five minutes, I can get an informative e-mail from them and then respond with a phone call or e-mail so my voice as a mother is heard.

Talk to your teenagers. What issues are they facing that may require outside resources?

A Mom's Prayer

Lord, help me be active, a mom with her ear to the ground and not her head in the sand. Help me equip my teen to be the one influencing others for positive change. Amen.

The Launching Pad

Giving Teens Wings to Fly

Cell phones have become markers on the road to independence. Like many moms, Candy gave her son a cell phone when he began to drive so she'd know where he was at all times and he'd have help in case of an emergency. She asked her son to call home if he would be out past his curfew. One Saturday night while waiting up for him, she dozed off in front of the TV. Later she woke to realize that there was no sign of him, and he had not called.

Irate, she punched in his number. When he answered, she demanded, "Where are you, and why haven't you bothered to call?"

"Mom," he sleepily replied, "I'm upstairs in bed. I've been home for an hour."

As long as you keep your sense of humor, launching a teen into independence can be fun and exciting.

What's Next?

We release our kids gradually, step-by-step, preparing them for the big release—moving out of the house and off to college or a career.

Choosing what to do after high school is probably one of the most vital decisions of a young person's life. Will he or she travel, work, or join the military? How about a junior college, internship programs, trade and technical schools, or a four-year private or public college? There is no one-size-fits-all plan.

Here's an interesting option many parents are not aware of. Many Bible schools, youth organizations, and conference centers offer year-long Bible programs. These are noncredentialed, ungraded studies, sometimes featuring retreat-like settings, wonderful fellowhip and service opportunities, and an environment that is conducive to spiritual growth. Hume Lake's Joshua Project and Cannon Beach Conference Center's Ecola Bible School are fine examples. I (Pam) heard of a small Bible college in Jackson Hole, Wyoming, that is right on the border of Yellowstone National Park. Skiing and snowboarding days are built into their program! YWAM offers training for those wanting a career in vocational ministry. Their headquarters is in Hawaii, and that is a big plus to many students!

If your students decide to live at home and work or attend junior college, their life should change somehow from their high school days. Let them take on more responsibility. Encourage them to pay for tuition and transportation. Reassess their fair share of household chores or family responsibilities. You'll probably decide to remove a curfew, but they should at least act like a good roommate and keep you abreast of their whereabouts and plans.

Planning for College

I (Jill) stood in a room with several other parents, talking about the rewards and challenges of parenting teenagers. The conversation soon turned to college applications. We began comparing our experiences and found that we all felt as if we had failed to properly prepare our children for the college admitting process.

Kids don't usually think about college in junior high, but that's really when they need to begin planning for their future. No, their grades don't count then, but their study skills do. They need to understand the importance of their grades beginning with the first semester of their freshman year. Kids and parents should keep these things in mind:

- *Your GPA (grade point average) is very important.* You can't get into just any college. Some are very competitive and require GPAs of 3.5 or higher.

- *GPAs and PSAT and ACT/SAT scores will affect tuition.* Many colleges offer scholarships based upon PSAT or ACT/SAT scores, GPAs, and class rank. The reduction in tuition can be substantial.

- *Senior grades don't count for GPA on first-year college applications.* Because you are applying during the fall of your senior year, your freshman, sophomore, and junior grades are the only ones that will be averaged to determine your GPA for college admission and scholarships. Don't let your GPA sag!

What can parents do to help their kids prepare for college? Here are some ideas:

- *Begin encouraging good study habits in grade school.* Get in the habit of having your children do their homework as soon as they get home from school or at some other set time every day.

- *Be involved in your children's schoolwork.* Attend parent-teacher conferences and be available to help with homework. Ask your kids to show you their schoolwork.

- *Set educational standards.* Share your vision for academic excellence. Set an example as a lifelong learner.

- *Be an advocate when necessary.* Let your kids know you'll help if a teacher is being unfair.

- *Don't be afraid to let them suffer some consequences as well.* Mistakes are opportunities to learn. Parents can extend encouragement and grace to kids, while helping them to learn responsibility, organization, and new concepts.

- *Begin looking at college possibilities during the freshman year.* Surf the Web together to check out college websites. Scan financial aid pages to help your children set educational goals for academic grants and scholarships. This will help them understand why it is important to take their education seriously.

Selecting a College

Here are some questions to discuss with your teens when they are choosing a college:

- What is the academic reputation of the college? Does it have a strong program in my major?

- How do I feel about the campus setting and distance from home? How safe would I feel on campus?

- What is the teacher-to-student ratio?

- What is the cost of tuition, books, room, and board?

- Am I required to live on campus, or is affordable housing near?

- Is the campus near any churches I would like to attend?

Your kids may also want to consider special programs, sports, extracurricular needs, or the Greek system. Brock created a matrix to decide where to attend college. He listed the factors that meant the most to him. Then he gave each factor a point value (five points for most important down to one point for lesser issues) and rated several colleges and universities. Here's a simple example:

		College			
		A	B	C	D
Academic reputation	(rate 1–5 and multiply by 4)	16	8	12	20
Strength of my major	(rate 1–5 and multiply by 5)	20	15	10	20
Campus setting	(rate 1–5 and multiply by 3)	15	15	9	12
Distance from home	(rate 1–5 and multiply by 1)	5	5	4	2
Cost: tuition and books	(rate 1–5 and multiply by 3)	9	12	15	9
Cost: room and board	(rate 1–5 and multiply by 3)	9	12	15	15
Local churches	(rate 1–5 and multiply by 5)	10	25	20	10
	Total	84	92	85	88

Soaring to Success

Discovering the path and moving your teen to the launching pad is an exciting adventure. Letting him or her go—now that's the hard part! Here are a few ways to release and yet stay connected.

Parties proclaim it. Going-away parties and graduation get-togethers help both you and your student adjust to the new path ahead. The Farrels and Savages have used campus tours, graduation parties, a dinner out with just Mom and Dad, a Moms In Touch graduates' prayer party, youth group graduates' trip, and an end-of-the-summer send-off. Each party or event helped us adjust to the life ahead for our graduates.

Messages make it real. A send-off letter or a graduation prayer, tells your teen you believe in his or her ability to fly out of the nest and succeed.

Boxes bring it on. Help your graduates pack up their room, or at least the parts they might take with them. Use these times to build the relationship. Instead of focusing on your potential loneliness, focus on their opportunity. As you help them pack, recall happy memories and identify positive traits. Use this time to reinforce the relationship.

Prayer prepares you both. Have your friends and family pray for you and your college student. Every parent reacts to the "drop off" day differently. Some moms and dads cry, and others are as excited as their children. Make sure the day has been bathed in prayer.

Packages for peace of mind. To avoid constant nagging, create a college care package that has answers to your biggest worries. I (Pam) included a couple devotionals, some Christian music CDs, a few CDs and DVDs with movies and teachings that were relevant to their life, books like *How to Stay Christian in College* and *The Incredible Four-Year Adventure.* and a bookmark with websites like www.boundless.org. An emergency calling card and an emergency 20-dollar bill helped ease my worries too.

The Freshman Foundation

We (the Farrels) believe preparation is the best method to gain success. We collated a *huge* amount of information we wanted to relay to our 18-year-olds and divided it into five key topics. We wrote questions that our kids could use to plan for success for the college years. We call this material the Freshman Foundation. If your teen is not going to college, rename these five keys the Graduate Groundwork. They are necessary for anyone to succeed in the adult world. We encourage parents and freshmen to set aside five coffee dates or five walks to go over these questions.

One of our sons joined me for walks on the beach five nights in a row. I took another son out to a series of five dinners. Both worked great. Most seniors are already thinking through these issues and questions, and they are relieved and grateful you care enough to discuss them. Visit www.masterfulliving.com to find questions you could use, and read on to see how we organized the concepts into five categories.

1. Fitness

We decided to start the Freshman Foundation with the least emotionally volatile topic—where to live and how to stay physically healthy. Your goal is to help your student choose an affordable environment in which he or she will thrive. Living at home for two years may not sound like fun, but completing a degree debt free is a huge benefit! If going away to college is an option financially, discuss factors that will lead to success physically, socially, academically, and spiritually.

One of our sons attended a junior college and rented a room from a family in the area we know. Another son thrived in an apartment with like-minded friends. Wherever students live, they need to consider getting enough sleep and carrying a health insurance card. A nice going-away gift is a supply of over-the-counter medications.

2. Finances

Review your student's income and expenses. How much scholarship money will be coming in each term? How much will you contribute? How much will he or she pay? Will he or she be getting loans? Grants? How much can he or she work and still achieve well in school? Studies have shown that those who work or are on athletic scholarships get higher grades than those who don't. You shouldn't work harder at your kids' education than they are willing to work. Plenty of sacrifice is good for college students as it helps them take ownership of their education.

Introduce the student to the campus financial aid office. Have him or her write a budget, which encourages tithing. *Money Management for College Students* is a helpful resource from Crown Financial Ministries. By now the student should have a checking account and a bank debit card. Have a conversation about credit ratings and how to build a strong one. Discuss if and when you would consider a loan, and if you would or would not ever cosign for him or her.

Clarify whether the money you contribute comes with any conditions. A money card is one of the most significant motivational tools you have as a parent. In our family, college is a privilege, not a right, so any help we give is tied to growth we see in our kids' moral, spiritual, and community life. We will not fund sin. Our young adults know that drinking, drug use, irresponsible behavior, sex outside of marriage, skipping church, and avoiding campus Christian groups are all reasons for us to withdraw our financial support. A decision to rebel is a statement that the young adult wants to do things his or her own way, and we will let them have the full responsibility and consequence of those choices and decisions.

3. Future

Talk with your student about career goals, internships, and work experience. Encourage him or her to take a personal inventory such as the Keirsey Temperament Sorter, the Myers and Briggs Type Indicator, or the DISC profile. Life Pathways by Crown Financial Ministries is a relatively inexpensive yet comprehensive inventory. Many colleges have career centers with software available to assess your preferences and suggest potential careers.

4. Friends

Relationships form the centerpiece of a college student's life. We talked with our sons about dating standards, finding friendships with people with similar values, and finding mentors and reliable leaders. We also discovered how our relationship with them was going to move from parent to friend over the next four years and how we were going to help facilitate this transition by turning more and more of the responsibility of their own life over to them. We also brainstormed ways to expand their social circle and spend more time with people from a variety of socioeconomic backgrounds, cultures, and countries.

5. Foundations

The most important discussion to have with your kids when they leave home will be about their spiritual decisions. How will they find a local church to attend and campus groups to join? Encourage your students to choose a church where they can serve and use their gifts.

This is also the time to ask your teenagers about their personal walk with God. Ask them to rate their devotional life. How is their daily quiet time? Bible study? Prayer life? Service? Instead of pointing out areas you believe they need to improve or change, encourage their ownership of this area of their life by asking where they need improvement and what their plan is to grow. Ask what you can do to assist them. One of our sons asked for Christian music to play in his truck and apartment. Another son wanted books to help him write papers defending his faith while attending a state university.

Walk with your young adults until they are solidly walking with God. Instead of nagging, make a commitment with your teenagers to always speak honestly about each of your spiritual lives, sharing how God is helping you grow. Share favorite verses you discover, share how God is convicting you of any shortcomings, share things that inspire you. Model an authentic vulnerability, and this will give permission to your teenagers to do the same, not just with you but with others in his or her world.

 ### *From the Heart*

As I wrote my contributions to this chapter, our second-oldest child, Evan, received the mail he's been waiting for: the college acceptance letter from his university of choice. Evan was so excited that I thought I was going to have to peel him off the ceiling. That lasted about an hour. Then it struck him—the reality of being six hours from home, the reality of living on his own, the reality of being away from family and friends. Our oldest son is launching into his college years.

During that same period of time our oldest daughter began having conversations with an American family living in France. They were discussing the possibilities of her moving overseas and becoming an *au pair* for their family. As I read the e-mail exchange between this couple (who are personal friends of our family) and my daughter, tears came to my eyes. My little girl isn't little anymore. She's launching into adulthood.

A mother's goal is to eventually work herself out of a job. When our children are preschoolers, we feel as if they will be little forever. During that season, a sense of accomplishment seems out of reach. That's because we're defining accomplishment by looking for short-term goals and tasks that stay finished for a while. But true accomplishment in the profession of motherhood requires more than 18 years. Sometimes the journey through the teen years is relatively smooth, and sometimes it's a challenge for both parent and teen.

Regardless of the nature of the journey, we don't have to make it alone. God walks with us and our children through their teen years. He promises we won't be alone and that if we'll trust Him, He'll give us the wisdom we need every step of the way.

Got teens? I do, and as challenging as it is, I love this season of motherhood. You and I have the privilege of loving our teens, leading them, and eventually launching them into lives of their own. I can't think of a better accomplishment than that!

The Next Step

What stage of release is your son or daughter in all the major areas discussed in this book? On the chart below, mark the place they are at in assuming responsibility in that area:

Communicating and resolving conflict
(chapter 1) 1   2   3   4   5

Finding his or her niche
(chapter 2) 1   2   3   4   5

Demonstrating life skills and people skills
(chapter 3) 1   2   3   4   5

Maintaining pure interpersonal relationships
(chapter 4) 1   2   3   4   5

Handling money and being a good steward
(chapter 5) 1   2   3   4   5

Being self-disciplined, self-directed, and teachable
(chapter 6) 1   2   3   4   5

Coping with the unwelcome or unwanted
(chapter 7) 1   2   3   4   5

Overcoming difficult emotions and obstacles
(chapter 8) 1   2   3   4   5

Relating to God on his or her own
(chapter 9) 1   2   3   4   5

Making a positive impact
(chapter 10) 1   2   3   4   5

Owning his or her life responsibly
(chapter 11) 1   2   3   4   5

A Mom's Prayer

*Lord, I release my graduates into Your care. I have done
all I can—now place them under Your wings. Help them
soar to success in all areas of life as they lean on You for
wisdom and understanding. Amen.*

Appendix

Got Teens? Discussion Questions

Note to leaders and facilitators: Moms of teens need ongoing encouragement. These discussion questions for each chapter of *Got Teens?* provide a structure for moms to study together, share their own needs, and pray. (At www.masterfulliving.com, you will find Bible-based prayers that you can use by inserting your own teen's name.)

Here's an idea that can get you started: Ask each member of the group to bring a photo of her teens to the first meeting. Each mom can then introduce her teens by sharing their first names and one positive quality about each one.

Our prayer is that as you network with other moms, you will find the encouragement and equipping you need to be the best mom you can be. For additional information on developing a successful moms' group, check out the Hearts at Home resource *Creating the Moms' Group You've Been Looking For* by Jill Savage.

Chapter 1—A Listening Ear

1. What did you learn from this chapter about the way teens think?

2. What transitions has your teen already experienced? What transitions are still ahead? What have you learned during a transition time?

3. What has helped you to communicate or resolve conflict with your teen? Do you currently need help resolving an issue with your teen?

4. Is your teen usually an inward thinker or outward speaker (an introvert or an extrovert)?

5. How might you choose to celebrate a significant moment in your teen's life?

6. Close the meeting by asking for prayer requests from the group and having a volunteer pray for them.

Chapter 2—Casting Vision

1. What resources listed in this chapter would be likely to be most helpful for your teen?

2. What is your teen's "role in the forest"? Identify one of your teen's strengths you can build on and one weakness you can pray about.

3. Brainstorm ways to encourage your teen to complete the uniqueness inventory. What incentives or words of affirmation might motivate your teen to complete the inventory?

4. What have you learned that helps you know how and where to draw the line with your teen?

5. Close by writing one prayer request for your teen on a 3 x 5 card. Exchange cards with another mom and pray for each other's teens all week.

Chapter 3—On Being a Mentor

1. What household tasks are your kids responsible for?

2. What life skills does your teen need to improve (for example, manners, cleaning, cooking, or laundry)?

3. What expectations or rules did you experience as a teen driver? What rules or guidelines do you have or will you have for your teen as a driver?

4. How can you help your teen to do the right thing?

5. Identify the specialists in your group, such as the cook, the computer whiz, or the authority on manners and etiquette. For your next meeting, find a helpful article, book, or some other training tool that other moms can learn from. Consider having each mom share one idea from her area of expertise or success during your next meeting.

Chapter 4—Becoming a Relationship Specialist

1. What is your biggest fear and your most exciting hope for your teen's relationships?

2. What one relational decision did you make as a teen that you hope your teen also makes?

3. What sex and dating trends in society or in your child's peer circle concern you?

4. What is the next step for you after reading this chapter?

5. How can you reward or celebrate your teen for setting his or her own relationship standards?

6. How can you get Dad involved in the conversation (or a safe male role model if Dad is not in the picture)?

7. Does your group want to create an evening to highlight the guy-girl relationship? Is there a young couple who you think is a good role model that you can invite to a dinner and interview? Is there a campus or church group that you can team with for a special activity to train students in relationship skills and standards?

Chapter 5—The CFO

1. What is your financial relationship with your teen? Does your teen receive an allowance, work at home for pay, or work outside the home?

2. Which of these do you need more training in so you can better equip your teen?

the value of a dollar	investing	sharing
budgeting	delaying gratification	diligence
saving	rest	accountability

3. Do you have a plan for financing your teen's higher education?

4. What did you learn from this chapter about financial stewardship? What step do you want to take in this area?

5. When have you experienced God's provision?

6. Close by praying for God's wisdom and provision for the person on your right.

Chapter 6—The Referee

1. What responsibility can you begin releasing to your teen?

2. What tips did you learn from this chapter that will help your teen make wise choices and be a person of integrity?

3. What creative correction ideas did you learn from this chapter?

4. How do people in your family say I'm sorry or give apologies? Do you need to begin apologizing to your teen in a new way? Does your teen need to learn how to apologize?

5. What has been the hardest issue for you and your teen to deal with? How have you handled it? What other resources have helped your teen make wise decisions?

6. What does God want to change in your own life so you can be a better example for your teen? Have each mom write a letter to God about a change she needs to make. After giving time to write the letter, close the meeting in prayer, praying for the person on your right.

Chapter 7—A Loving Shepherd

1. How have you helped a child in physical or emotional pain? What helped you find the strength to help your child?

2. Many ideas are listed in the chapter to develop a support system for your family. Do you have a strong support system? Do you need one? What steps might you take to develop or strengthen your support system?

3. Has God led you to a resource your teen needed?

4. What emotional issue in your teen's life do you want to pray about and look for a creative encouragement for?

5. Some of the moms in the book had to let their children go because of death. What did you learn from their stories than can help you today?

6. In pairs, share prayer requests and pray for each other. Pray that God would give you the strength, stamina, and courage needed to raise your teen.

Chapter 8—A Life Preserver

1. Were you rebellious or on the edge when you were a teen? Why do you think you made the choices you did?

2. Tim Kimmel lists many reasons why teens rebel. What insight into teens did you learn from reading this chapter? Which reason for rebellion do you think is most common in your experience?

3. Did you learn anything new about encouraging a wounded or broken heart? Does God want you to do something for your teen?

4. Six Statements of Forgiveness are included in this chapter. Bitterness inhibits our ability to be effective parents. Is God is asking you to forgive anyone?

5. What did you learn from this chapter about reconciling relationships?

6. Spend time this week praying the suggested Scripture-based prayers in this chapter over the life of each teen represented in the group.

Chapter 9—A Pastor at Home

1. What adult (besides you or your husband) has the most influence on your teen?

2. How might you build a relationship with a youth pastor or youth worker?

3. What local youth groups, campus clubs, or other organizations are available to help your teen?

4. Has your teen gone on a missions trip? How did it affect his or her life?

5. Does your teen spend time with God daily? Do you? How might you encourage the members of your family to develop their relationship with God and His Word?

6. Close by having each mom identify a resource that she has used to help her grow with God.

Chapter 10—The Social Activist

1. What issue in society is most likely to have a negative impact on your teen?

2. Have you ever taken action on a social issue? Did your action affect the situation? Did it affect you?

3. What new resource did you learn about in this chapter?

4. How do determine your family's standards for movies and other social activities?

5. Has your teen ever been involved in an unhealthy relationship or activity? How did you respond?

6. What can your group do to make a positive impact in your neighborhood?

7. Plan a special "launching pad" graduation for your moms' group as you close this study the next time you meet.

Chapter 11—The Launching Pad

1. When has letting go been the hardest for you?

2. How do you feel about sending your teen to college, to a trade school, or into the workplace? How will you prepare for the release?

3. How will you help your teen choose the next step after high school?

4. Does your teen have hopes and dreams for the future? How can you help your teen identify a dream and make a plan to achieve it?

5. Consider the five areas of the Freshman Foundation. In which area is your teen least prepared?

6. Which item in the chart at the end of the chapter represents your most pressing need? Your teen's most pressing need?

7. Practice releasing and affirming by selecting a fun or meaningful activity for your group to bring your study to a close. How might you celebrate what God has done for you as moms?

8. Close by praying for each other and your teens. Make sure to thank and praise God for any growth you have seen in yourself or your teen.

Notes

Chapter 1—A Listening Ear

1. Quotes in this section are taken from Brooks Craft Corbis, "What Makes Teens Tick," *Time*, May 10, 2004, p. 59.
2. Susan Alexander Yates, *And Then I Had Teenagers* (Grand Rapids: Baker Books, 2001), p. 69.
3. www.familylife.com/1-800-358-6329/detail.asp?id=8447

Chapter 2—Casting Vision

1. Susan Alexander Yates, *And Then I Had Teenagers* (Grand Rapids: Baker Books, 2001), p. 79.

Chapter 4—Becoming a Relationship Specialist

1. T. Suzanne Eller, *Real Issues, Real Teens* (Colorado Springs: Life Journey, 2004), pp. 53, 60.
2. Ibid., p. 54.
3. Ibid., p. 64.
4. www.doreenhanna.org/dotk
5. Steven Arterburn, et al., *Every Young Man's Battle* (Colorado Springs: Waterbrook Press, 2002).

Chapter 5—The CFO

1. Ellie Kay, *Money Doesn't Grow on Trees* (Bloomington, MN: Bethany House Publishers, 2002).
2. Debbie Nooffsinger, "Making Allowances," *Christian Parenting*, winter 2003, p 39.
3. Ibid., p. 40.

4. Todd and Lynn Zastrow, "Teaching Your Children About Money," *Hearts at Home*, October 2004, p. 24.

Chapter 6—The Referee

1. Lisa Welchel, *Creative Correction* (Wheaton, IL: Tyndale House Publishers, 2000), p. xv.

Chapter 7—A Loving Shepherd

1. Dana Serrano Chisholm is the founder and director of the Women's Resource Network.

Chapter 8—A Life Preserver

1. Tim Kimmel, *Why Christian Kids Rebel* (Nashville: W Publishing Group, 2004).
2. By Dick Eastman. © 1988, Every Home for Christ. Adapted by Moms In Touch. Used by permission.

Dear Readers,

We hope you have enjoyed this resource designed to encourage you in the profession of motherhood. We've worked to give you a great book with a lot of practical information to encourage and equip you in your motherhood journey through the teen years. We both speak and have other written resources to encourage you. To find out more about our speaking or writing you can contact us at our respective website and e-mail addresses:

Pam Farrel
website: www.masterfulliving.com
e-mail: mliving@sbcglobal.net

Jill Savage
website: www.jillsavage.org
website: www.hearts-at-home.org
e-mail: jillannsavage@yahoo.com

We'd love to know how *Got Teens?* has encouraged you! Drop us a line if you have a chance. May God bless you on your parenting journey, and may you always keep your heart at home.

Joining you in the journey,
Pam and Jill

The Hearts at Home organization is committed to meeting the needs of women in the profession of motherhood. Founded in 1993, Hearts at Home offers a variety of resources and events to assist women in their jobs as wives and mothers.

Find out how Hearts at Home can provide you with ongoing education and encouragement in the profession of motherhood. In addition to this book, our resources include the Hearts at Home magazine, the Hearts at Home devotional, and our Hearts at Home website. Additionally, Hearts at Home events make a great getaway for individuals, moms' groups, or for that special friend, sister, or sister-in-law. The regional conferences, attended by over ten thousand women each year, provide a unique, affordable, and highly encouraging weekend for the woman who takes the profession of motherhood seriously.

Hearts at Home
900 W. College Avenue
Normal, Illinois 61761
Phone: (309) 888-MOMS
Fax: (309) 888-4525
E-mail: hearts@hearts-at-home.org
Web: www.hearts-at-home.org

Two other great Hearts at Home books from Harvest House Publishers:

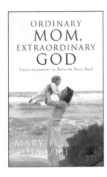

Ordinary Mom, Extraordinary God is a devotional aimed at the deeper issues of the heart and one that will provide a soothing respite amid chaos. Think of it as Oswald Chambers meets Busy Housewife.

Writer, speaker, and stay-at-home mom Mary DeMuth creatively focuses on the gift of motherhood as she considers...

- resting quietly in the Lord, even on crazy-busy days
- being thankful for the duties as well as the joys of being a mom
- offering God a heart to prune so that it can continue to bear good fruit

Personal stories integrated with scriptural truth and probing prayers will help you remain connected to the most amazing and extraordinary Parent of all parents.

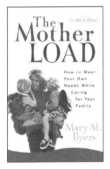

Motherhood is an intense, 'round-the-clock job. To stay healthy and happy, you need friends, laughter, solitude, balance, and an intimate relationship with the Lord. But exactly how do you meet these needs while juggling family responsibilities? Mary Byers, the mother of two lively young kids, shares how you can find small pockets of time to...

- rest and refuel
- create personal space
- make time for friendship, exercise, and intimacy
- identify and prevent "balance busters" that create chaos
- creatively stay sane in the midst of mothering

The Mother Load offers down-to-earth suggestions, spiritual truths, and real-life advice from moms to help women survive and thrive in today's active families. Includes questions for group discussion and personal reflection.

Other Hearts at Home Books

Professionalizing Motherhood
Jill Savage

So what do you do? Jill Savage assures women that motherhood is, indeed, a viable and valuable career choice. This rerelease of Hearts at Home's first book includes questions for reflection and a leader's guide. Quanity discounts available—call 1-309-888-MOMS.

Is There Really Sex After Kids?
Jill Savage

Having children in the home alters the sexual dynamic between husband and wife. *Is There Really Sex After Kids?* is written by a mom, for moms, and is filled with practical ideas. It is a woman-to-woman discussion—a true insider's look at what works to build intimacy outside the bedroom and improve intimacy inside the bedroom. Quantity discounts available—call 1-309-888-MOMS.

Creating the Moms Group You've Been Looking For
Jill Savage

This valuable resource manual provides moms with everything they need to know to start and improve effective moms ministries. This book has three primary purposes: To supply women with the vision and 'how-to' of starting a moms group, to serve as a consultation manual for women already in a group who want to know how to take their group or their leadership to the next level, and to provide church leaders with a comprehensive view of a mother's ministry.

Facing Every Mom's Fears
Allie Pleiter

Our world is only getting more frightening. *Facing Every Mom's Fear* shows mothers how to recognize when their fears are out of proportion. With tender humor and encouraging insights, author Allie Pleiter helps women thrive in the paradox of being protector, encourager, and comforter all at the same time. This book is ideal for personal use, group discussions, and mentoring relationships. Questions for personal reflection are included as well as a leader's guide with discussion starters.